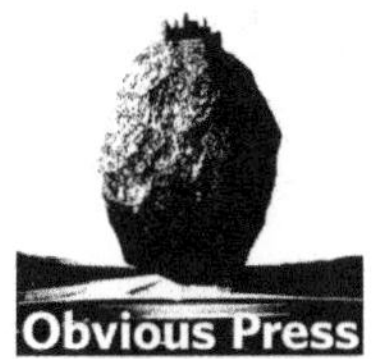

Undergraduate Work 1986-1989
University of Florida
Department of Architecture

Michael W. Muecke

Obvious Press
922 5th Street
Ames, IA, 50010-5906
USA
www.obviouspress.com

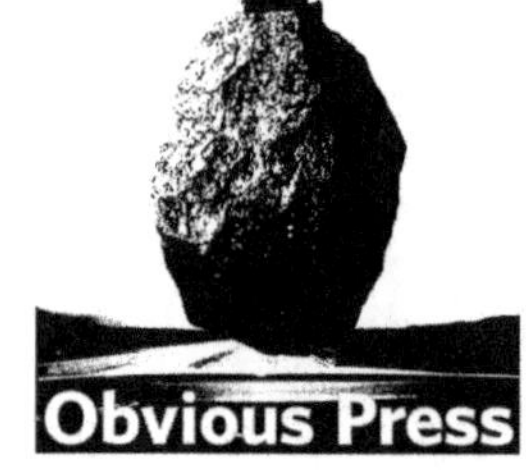

First published in 2017
MICHAEL W. MUECKE UNDERGRADUATE WORK 1986-1989.

For information address Obvious Press, 922 5th Street, Ames, IA 50010-5906 or write to editor@obviouspress.com

Paperback facsimile edition

ISBN-13: 978-1-941892-34-3
ISBN-10: 1-941892-34-5

Graphic design, layout, and typesetting by polytekton.com

Table of Contents

Introduction

The following pages contain design projects I completed between the fall of 1986 and the spring of 1989 in the Bachelor of Design program with a Major in Architecture at the University of Florida.

I used the portfolio as part of my application for the MArch program.

The work is situated at the watershed between analog and digital production. Computers were just about to be introduced into the design field at the University of Florida, and in my MArch design studios (1989-1991) I would use ArchiCad on Macintosh computers extensively; but in this case all drawings were done in either ink on mylar, pencil, or ink wash, and every model was made and assembled by hand.

The choice of font is testimony to this early engagement with computers: I had access to a Macintosh for the text blocks but my understanding of fonts was admittedly very rudimentary, so Times it was...

As I did the layout and assembled the pages I became increasingly more adventurous in connecting projects across different pages by treating the gutter as a link rather than a separator—as in the Savannah School of Design—to the point that the even the margins become connectors between projects, as in the Center for Latin-American Scholars.

We were also encouraged to include process in our portfolio, so the reader of these pages will notice many sketches and freehand diagrams that try to communicate the process of developing the designs.

The absence of good printing choices necessitated a trip to the photocopy machine (black & white, of course), and a facsimile of one of these runs is included here on pages 40-71. The increased contrast and the disappearance of grey tones is a typical byproduct of this process.

The aesthetics are based on a dynamic balance between space and object. A grid based on the golden section—dividing the original 8.5" square into smaller and smaller proportional dimensions—became the foundation used for the placing of images and text, with various adjustments, of course.

Both text and images are too close to the edge for comfort (there is no full bleed in photocopying;—) but the resulting contrast is worth it...

Facsimile of Original Paste-Up on Card Stock

Images and text blocks are pasted on the paper with rubber cement. Crude but effective.

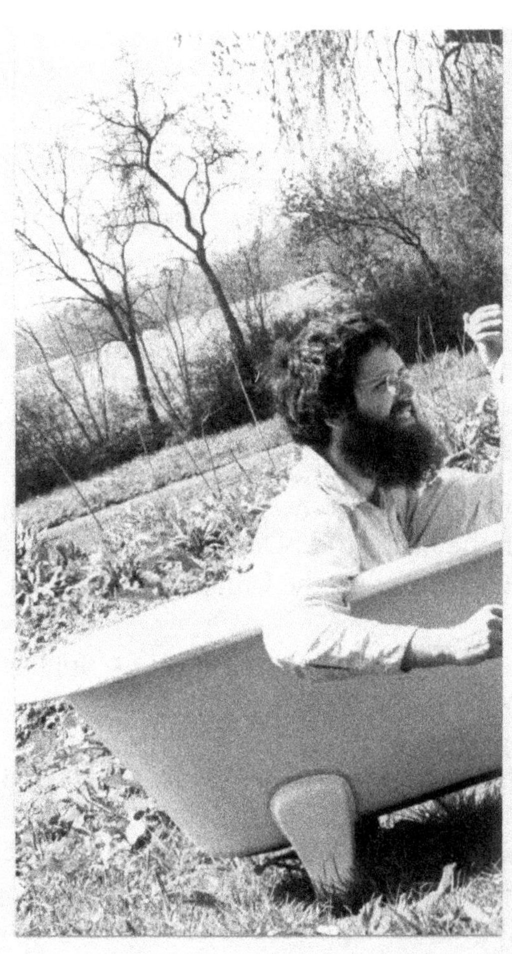

Michael Walter

8.5 in.

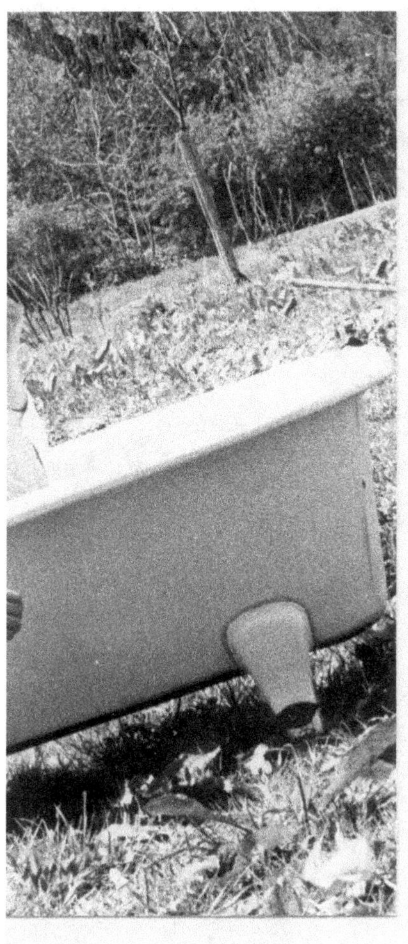

Mücke

1986-1989
undergraduate work

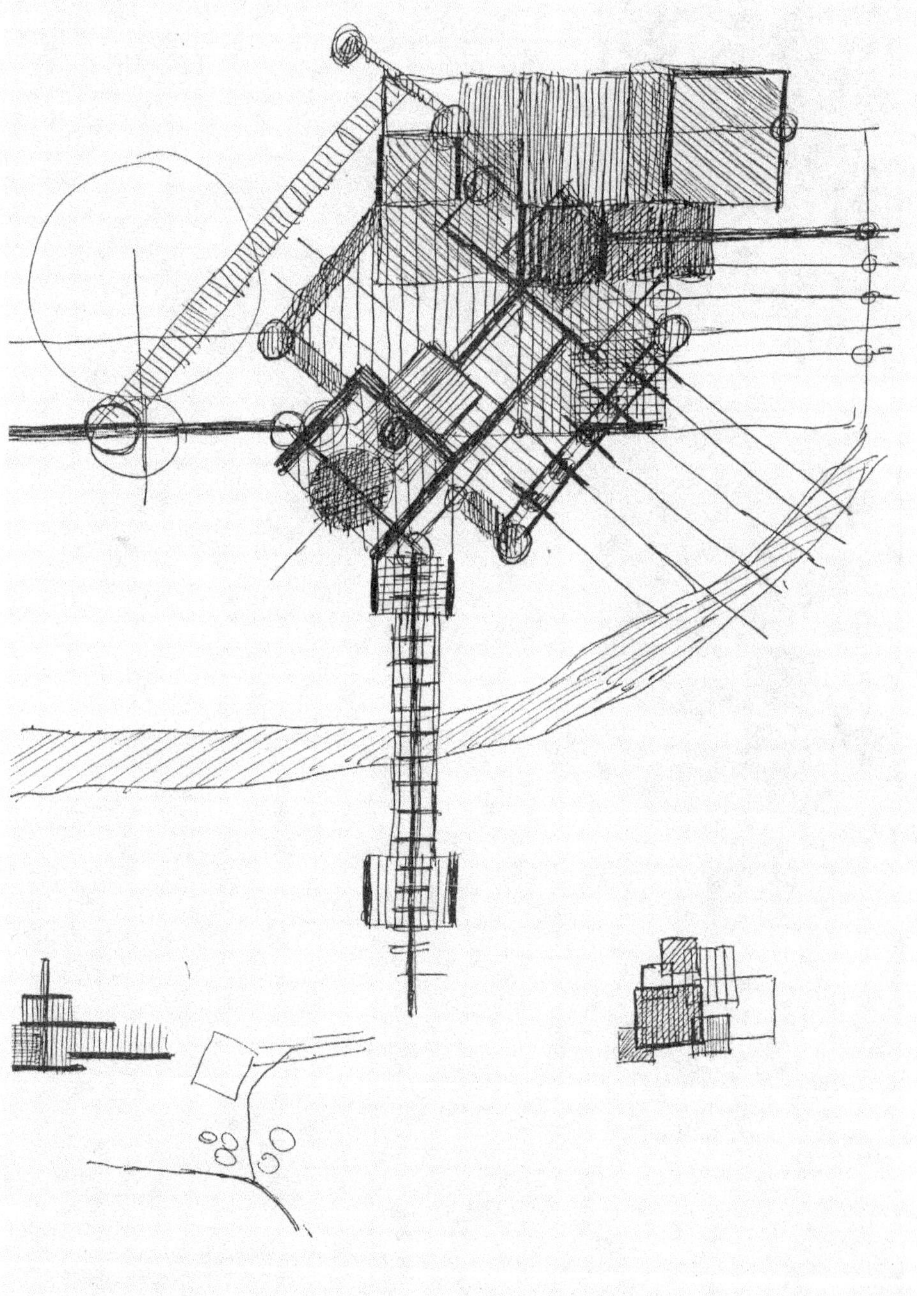

Gate House

Addirondack Mountains, New York Design 3

The gate house creates an entry to a villa on the other side of the bridge. This villa was built by Adolf Loos. Thus I appropriated Loos' ideas on architecture for the design of the gate house. The major characteristics include the following: carved space, design from inside out, and Raumplan, a name coined by Loos for his 'space-plan' design, i.e. interrelated but differentiated spaces.
The building itself is conceived as a frame with a massive central core which marks the turning point of the approach. This shift in direction also indicates a horizontal change from public to private functions. The building displays a 'closed' face towards the public access side (roadway with bridge) and opens up in the more private part towards nature.

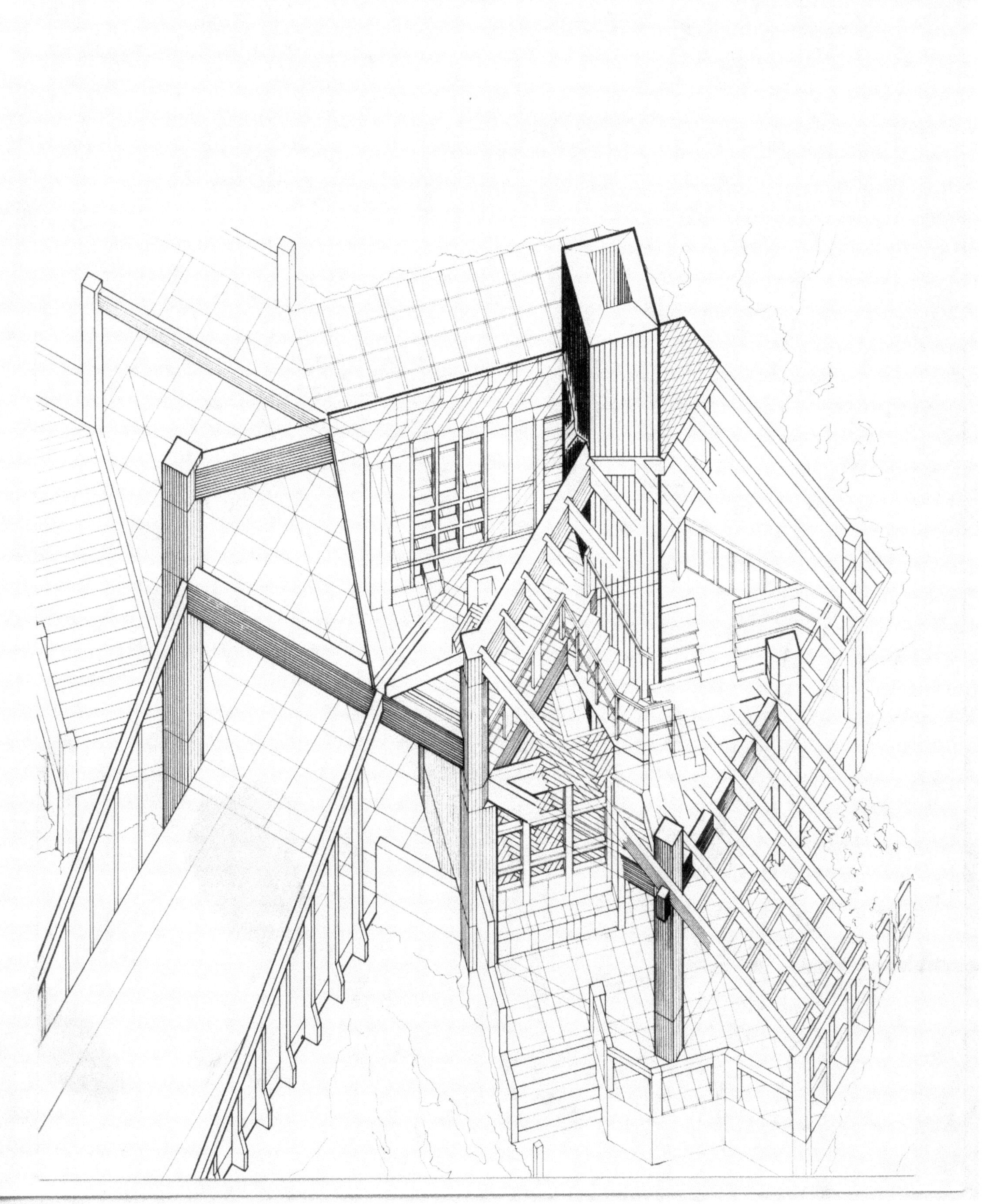

Monument to Commemoration and Condemnation

Design 4

Deconstructivism as theory base.

"Deconstruction is not a method, but a form of consciousness to some object."

<u>Commemoration:</u>
to serve as a memento or reminder; to honor the memory of by some observance or celebration.
<u>Condemnation:</u>
to pronounce adverse judgement on; to declare incurable.

Both ideas for this monument address thought or memory, and both can be viewed as intangible qualities. Thus the monument can not be occupied physically but only mentally. It can not be built, hence it is not a monument. Yet it can exist as a sign which refers to the real thing. Two deconstructed cubes, one in the ground, the other above ground, separated by a glass plate that allows visual access but prevents concrete experience.

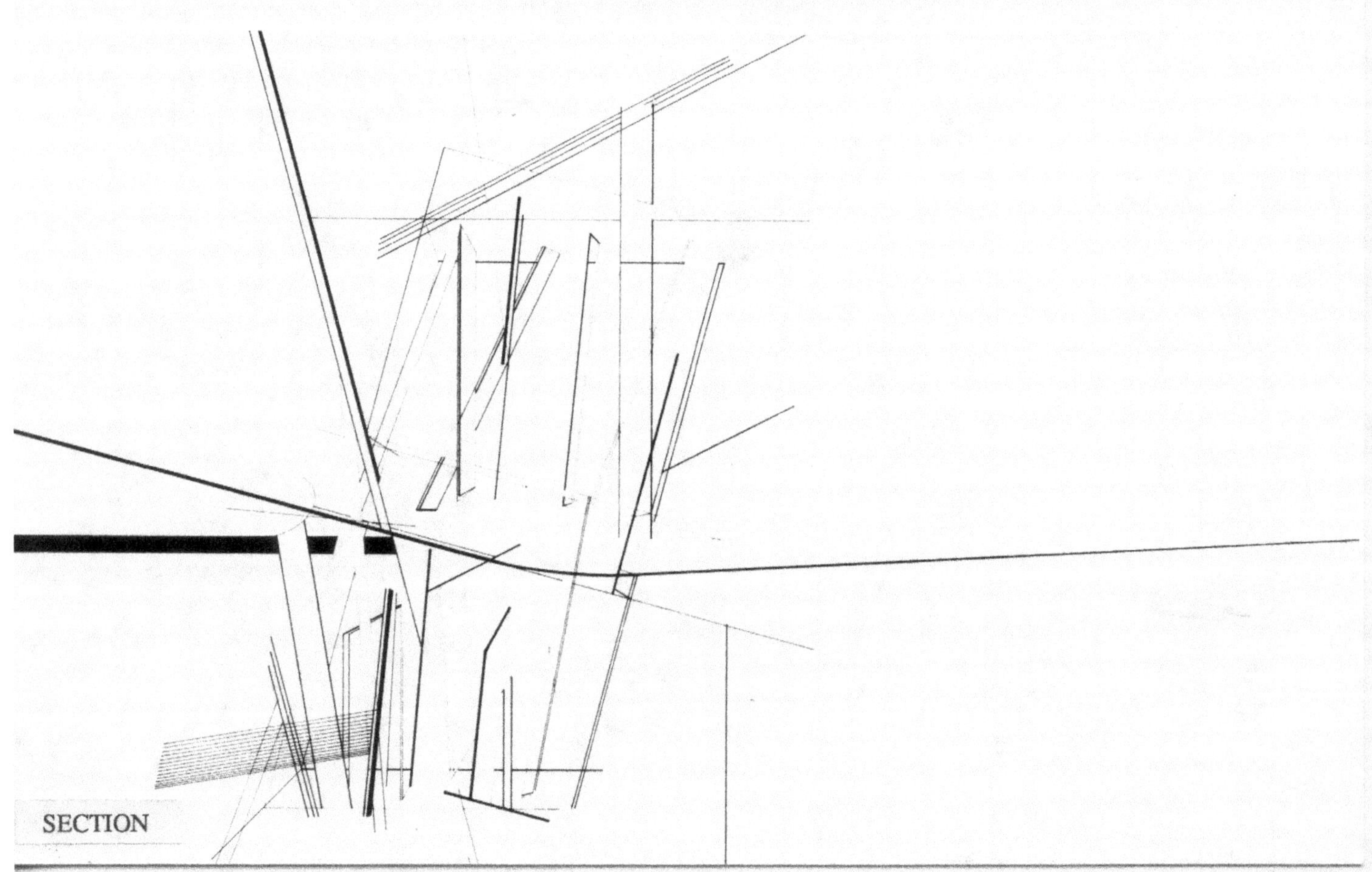

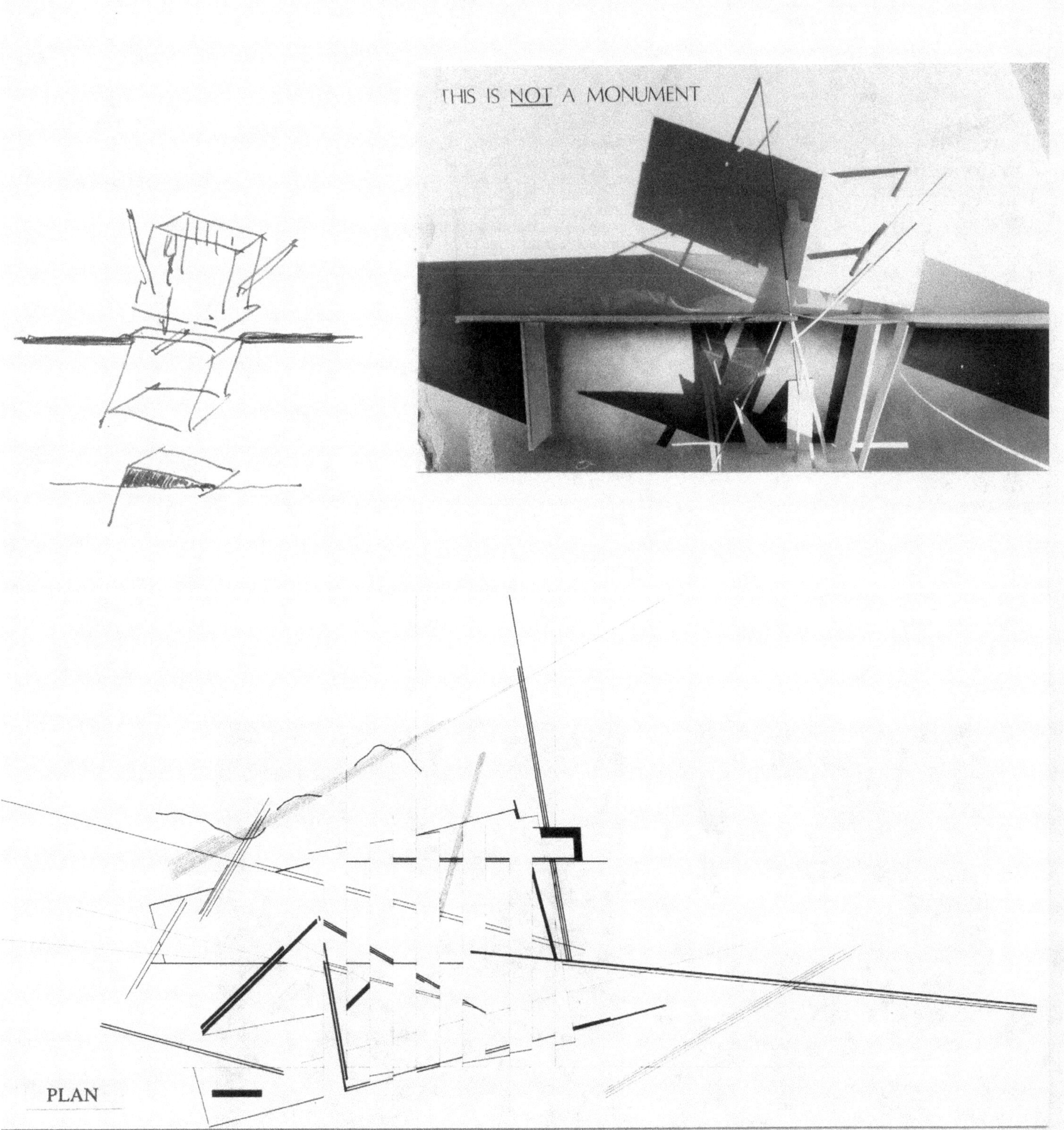
THIS IS NOT A MONUMENT
PLAN

Tower for Observation and Contemplation

Design 4

Project Parts:
1. Rolling hills.
2. Tower with
3. Observation space,
4. Meditation space,
   and
5. Path that connects both spaces.

Ideas:
tower
vertical,
to observe,
look into outside world.
to meditate,
look into inside world.
duality,
expansion of space
light
open
contraction of space
dark
closed.

For this project I studied the theory base of De Stijl which originated in the Netherlands. Subsequently I decided to investigate the idea of tower in terms of the DeStijl theory but also in concrete terms as a windmill. The two distinct spaces became two elevator boxes connected with a steel cable. If the observation space moves up the meditation space moves down and vice versa. The whole building can be turned to allow for viewing in all directions. In order to escape the dilemma of a purely orthogonal architecture the exit out of the tower is managed via an s-shaped slide.

STUDY MODELS

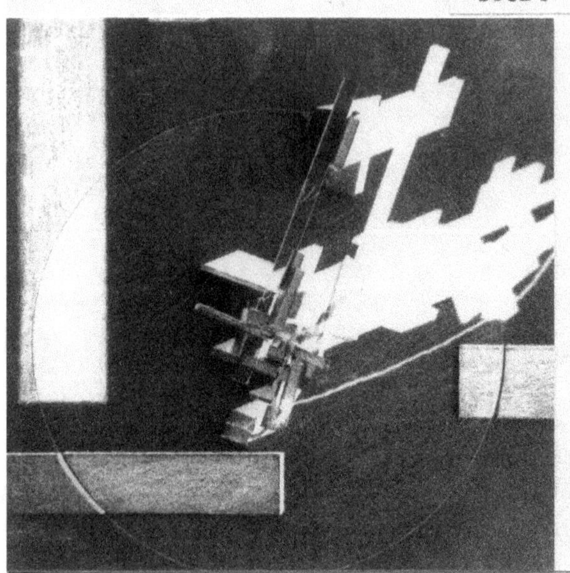

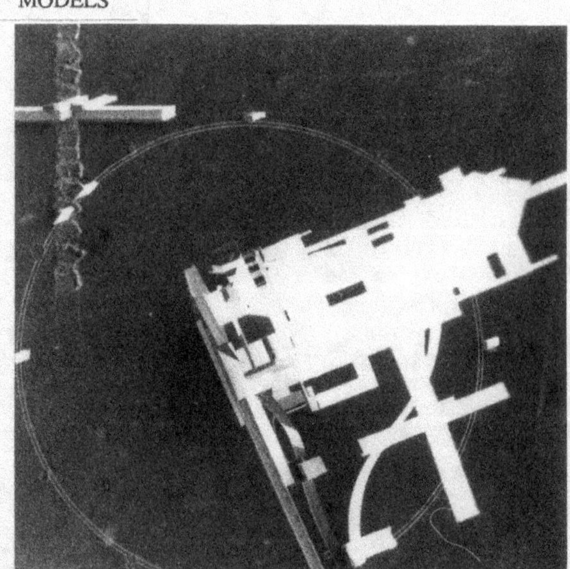

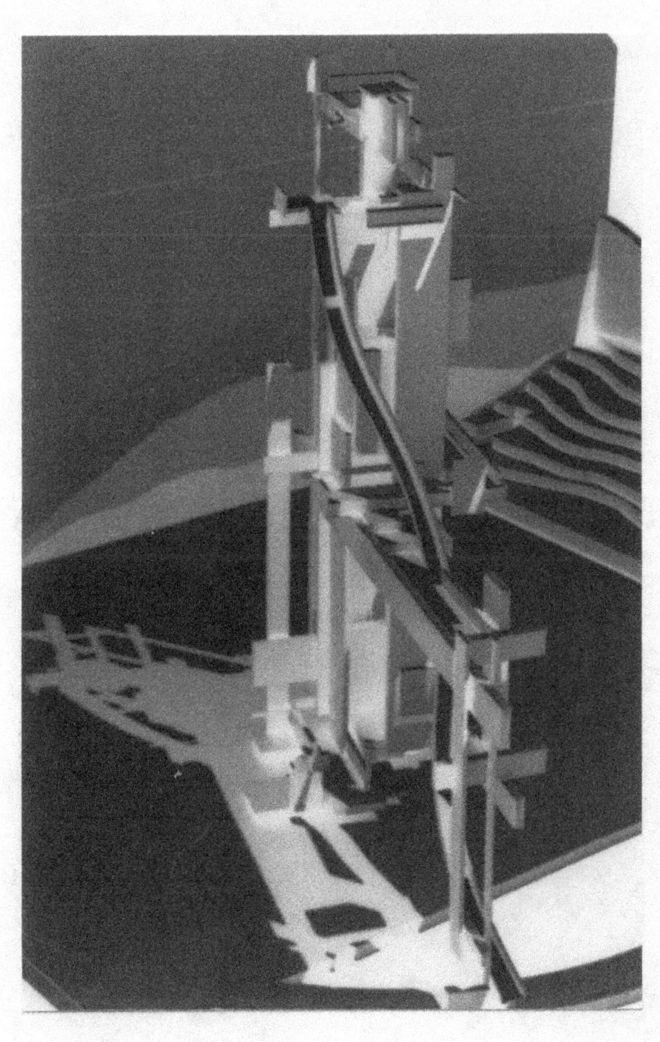

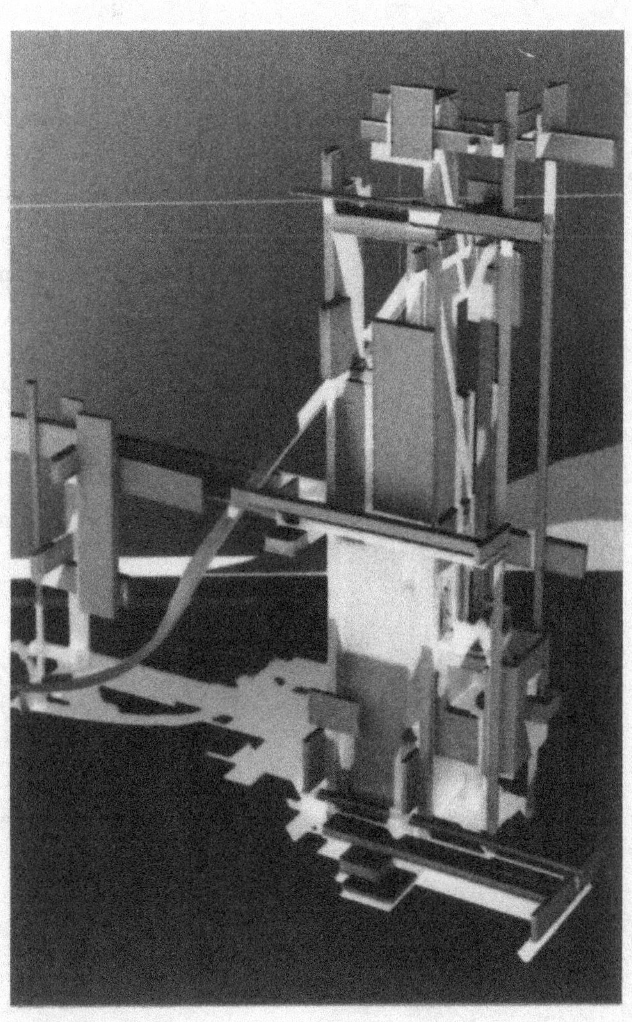

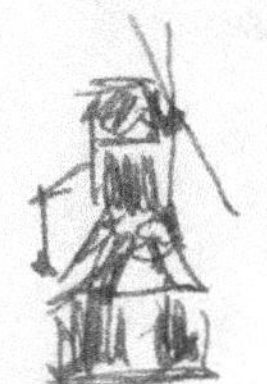

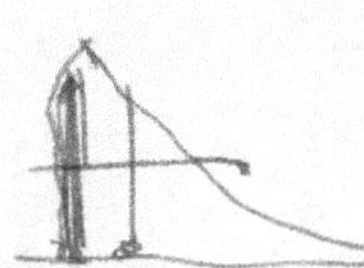

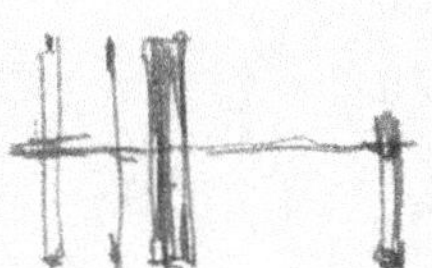

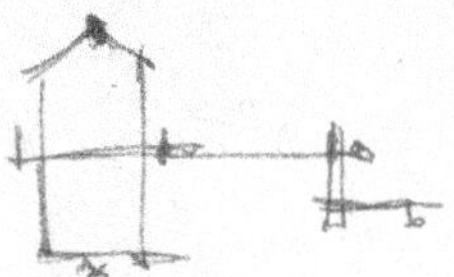

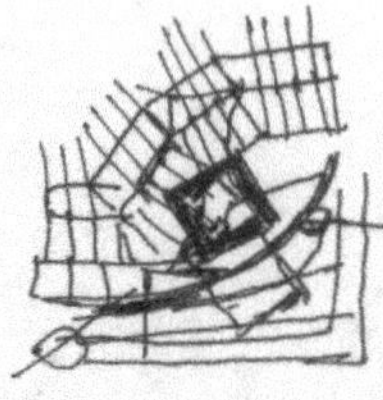

Center for Latin-American Scholars

Lake Alice, Gainesville
Design 3

At one scale the building complex creates a joint between Lake Alice and Museum Road. At another scale the central courtyard joins the two major programmes: private apartments which grow finger-like into the lake and public activities (auditorium, offices) which are adjacent to the more public realm, the street. The whole building complex becomes the meeting ground between nature and man-made nature while the courtyard creates a meeting place for different cultures. Even the layout for the individual apartments reflects on the micro scale the concept of joint and center. Here the stairs create a joint between the different spaces in the apartment.

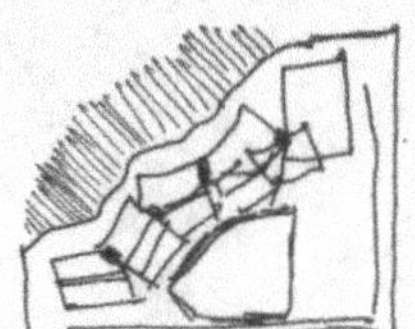

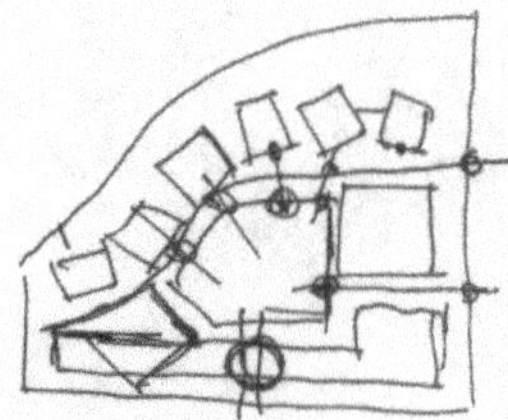

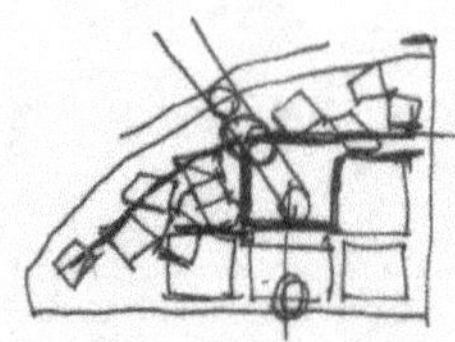

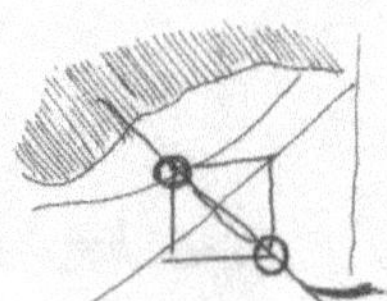

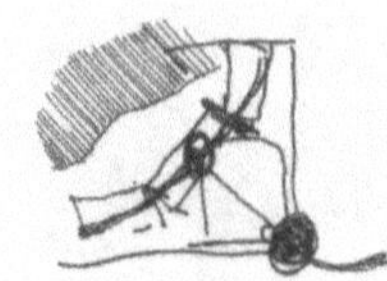

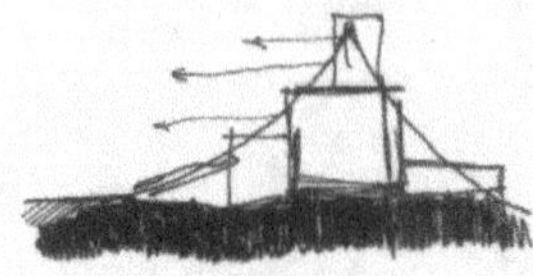

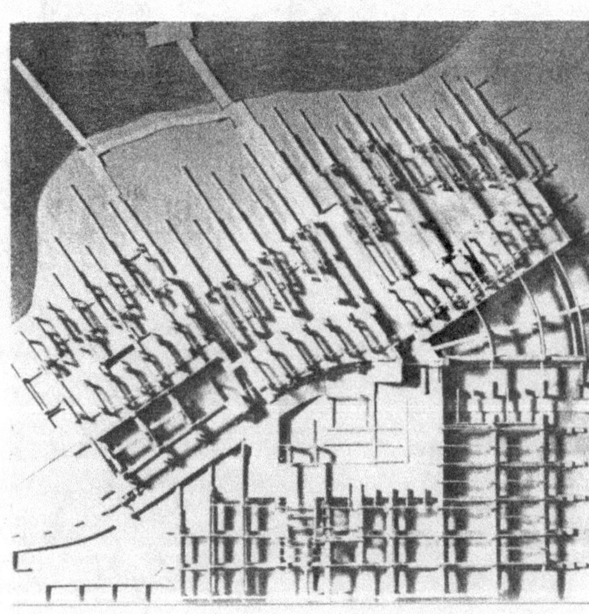

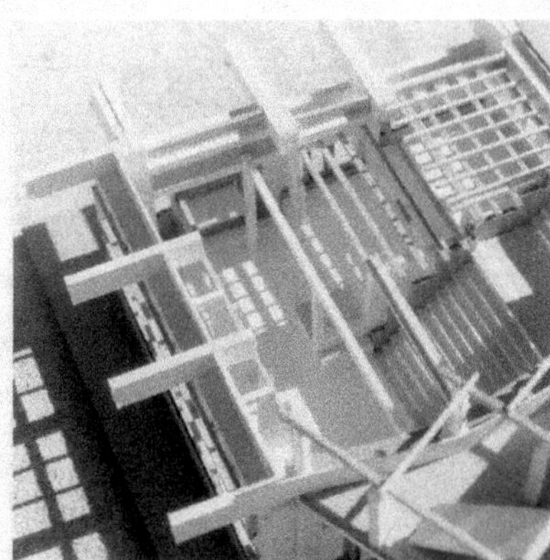

CENTRAL

COURTYARD

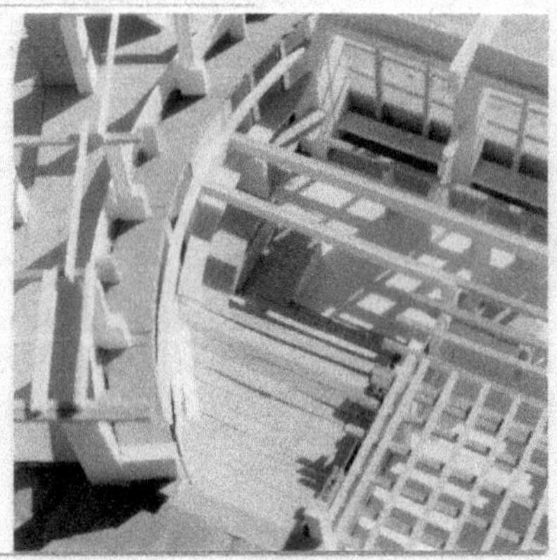

TYPICAL

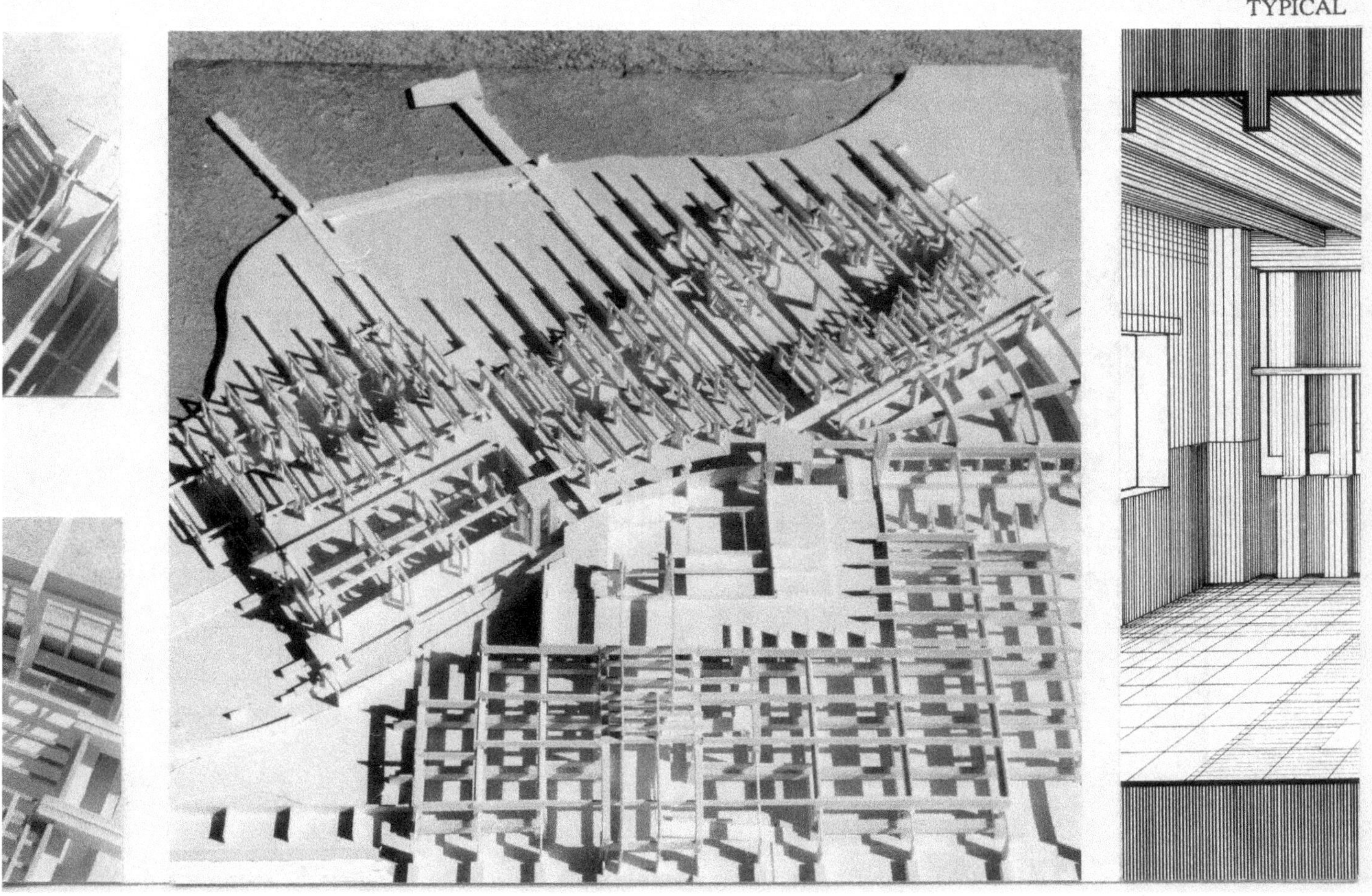

APARTMENT INTERIOR

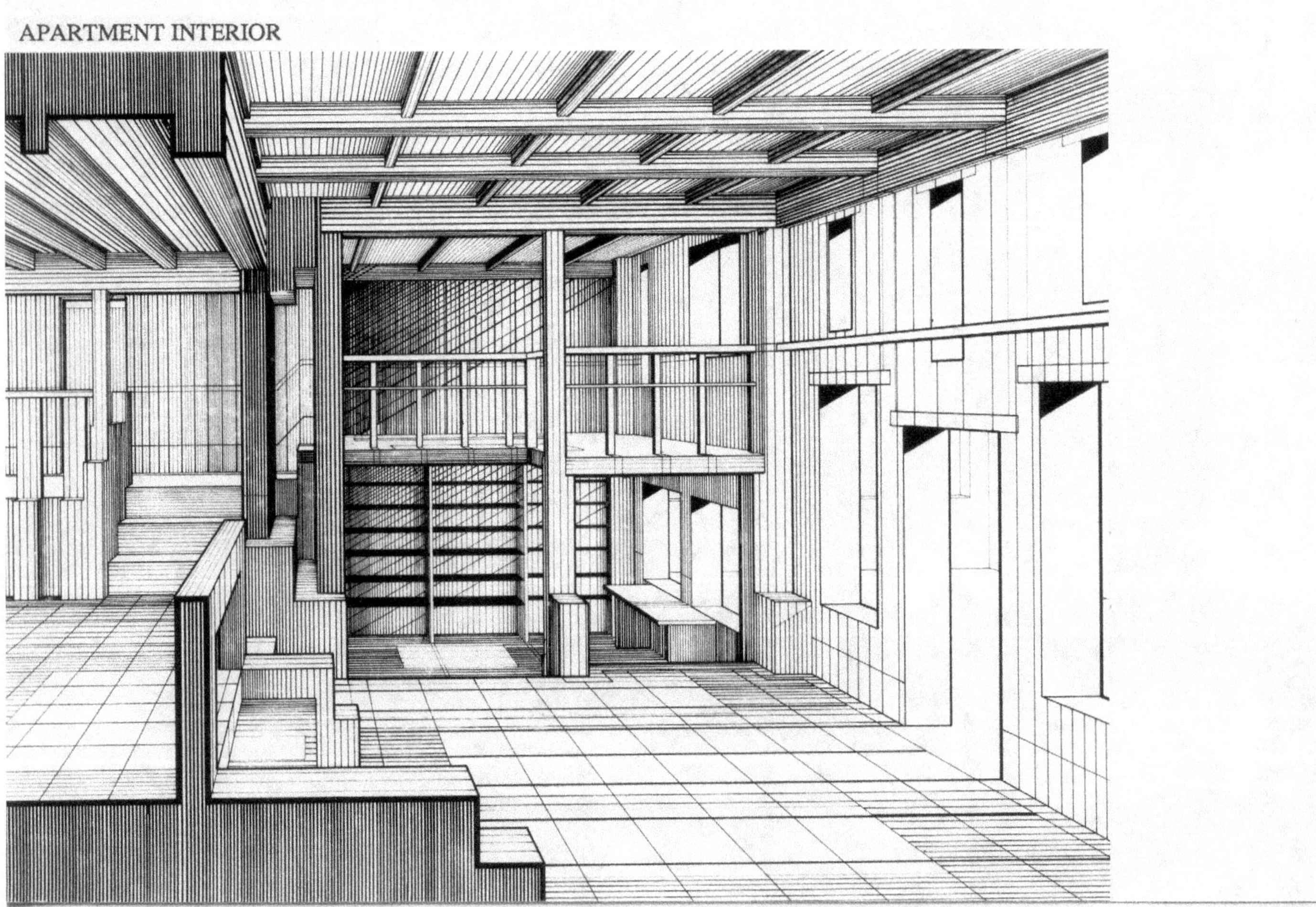

Savannah School of Design

Design 4

I arrived at the design for this project through the study of Savannah's architectural typology which include the ideas of the square, the walled street, and the inherent duality in the Savannah house.

The Design School is sited on one of the set piece lots fronting Monterey Square. Thus the building has a definite front addressing the square and a back oriented towards one of the through-streets. The sides of the building where kept as solid as possible to address the street as a space without becoming oppressive. For example an arcade runs around the southwest corner of the building to mediate between street and built environment.

The Design School itself is conceived as a tri-partite scheme. An object surrounded by space (studios and galleries) and space carved out of an object (dorms and offices) separated by a meeting space (cafeteria) which in Savannah's typology becomes the separator between servant's housing and owner's quarters.

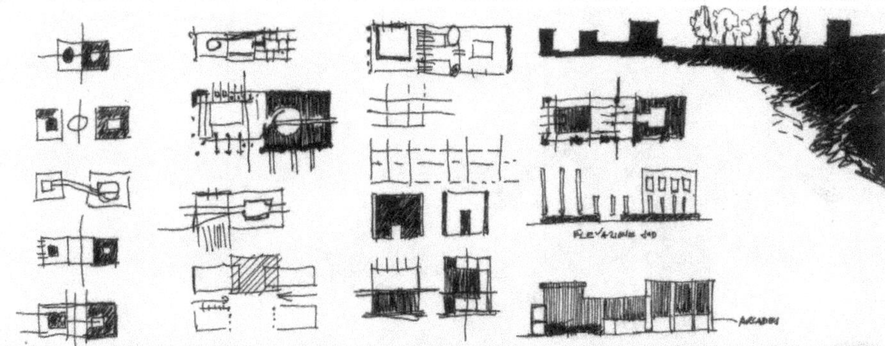

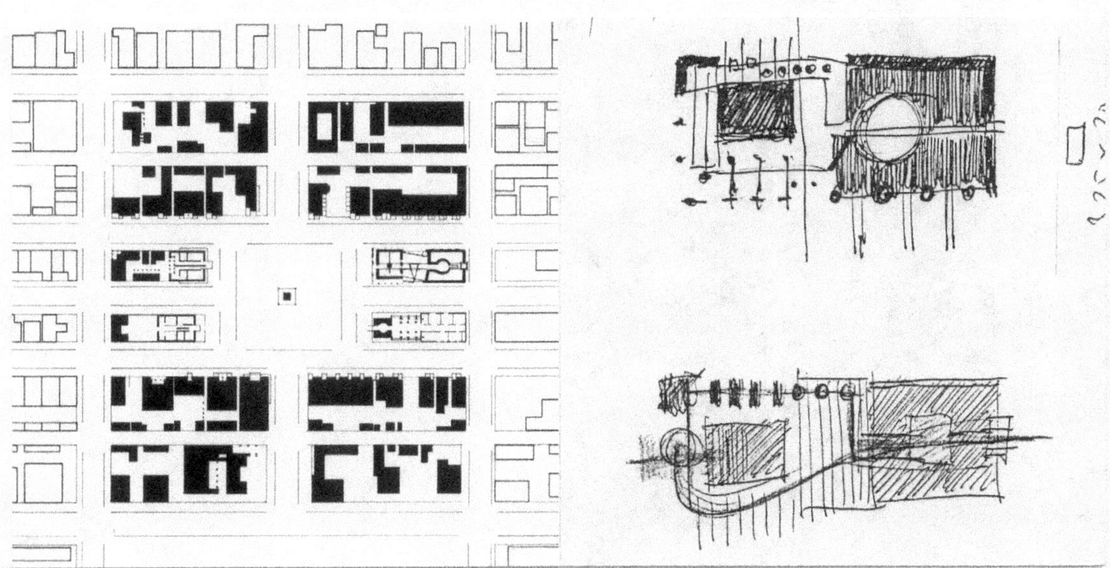

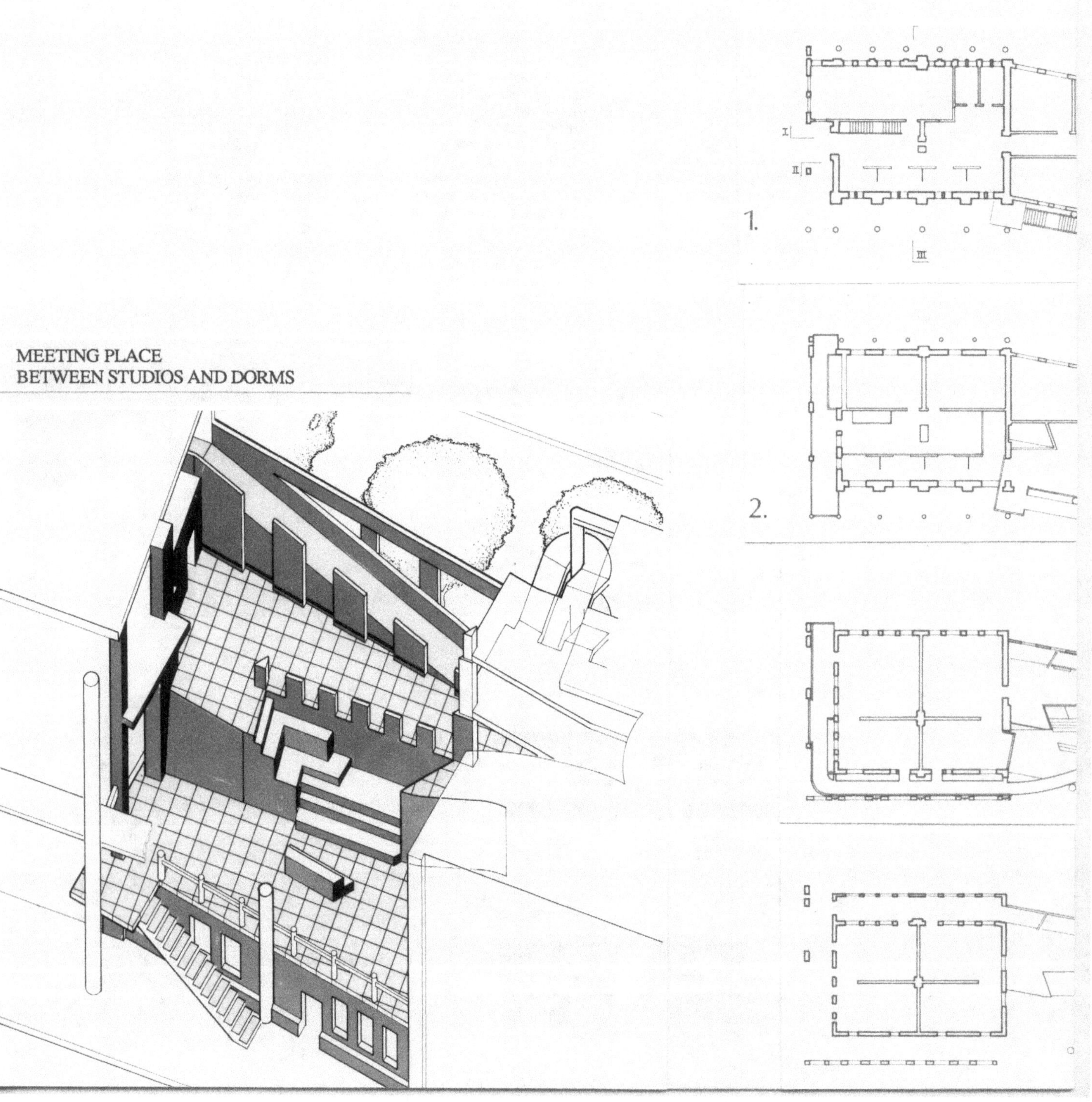

MEETING PLACE
BETWEEN STUDIOS AND DORMS

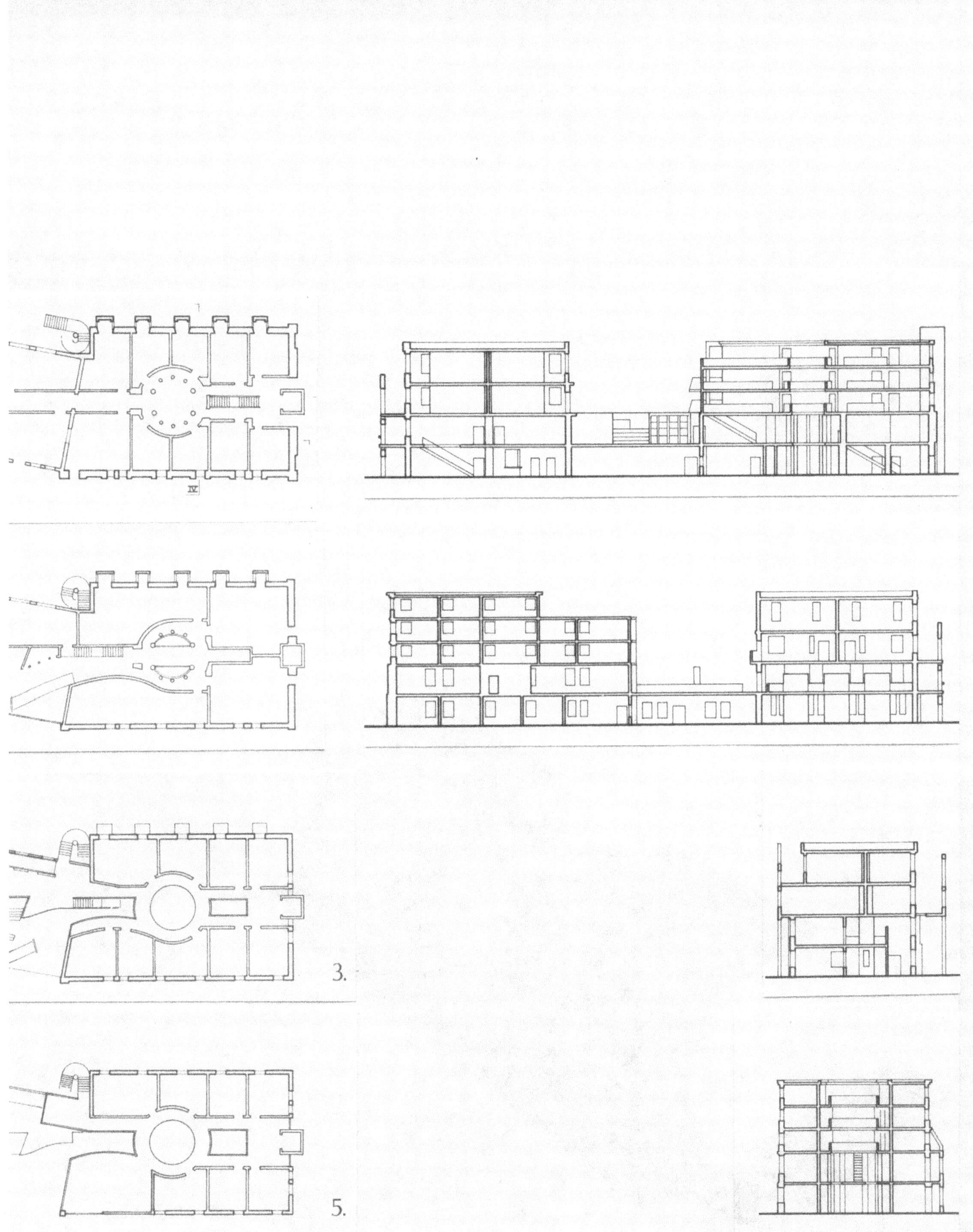
IV
3.
5.

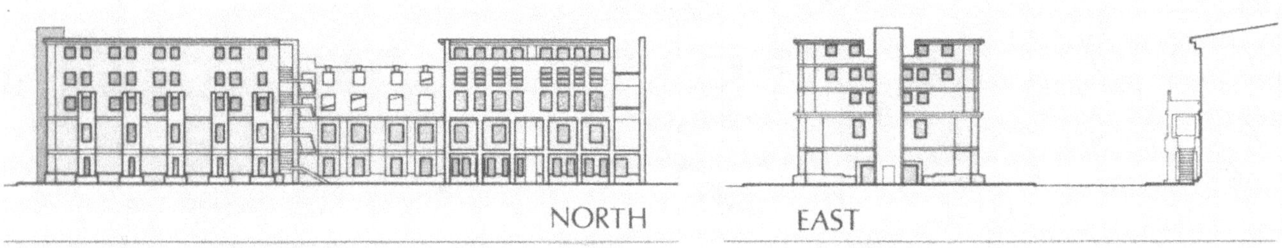
NORTH
EAST

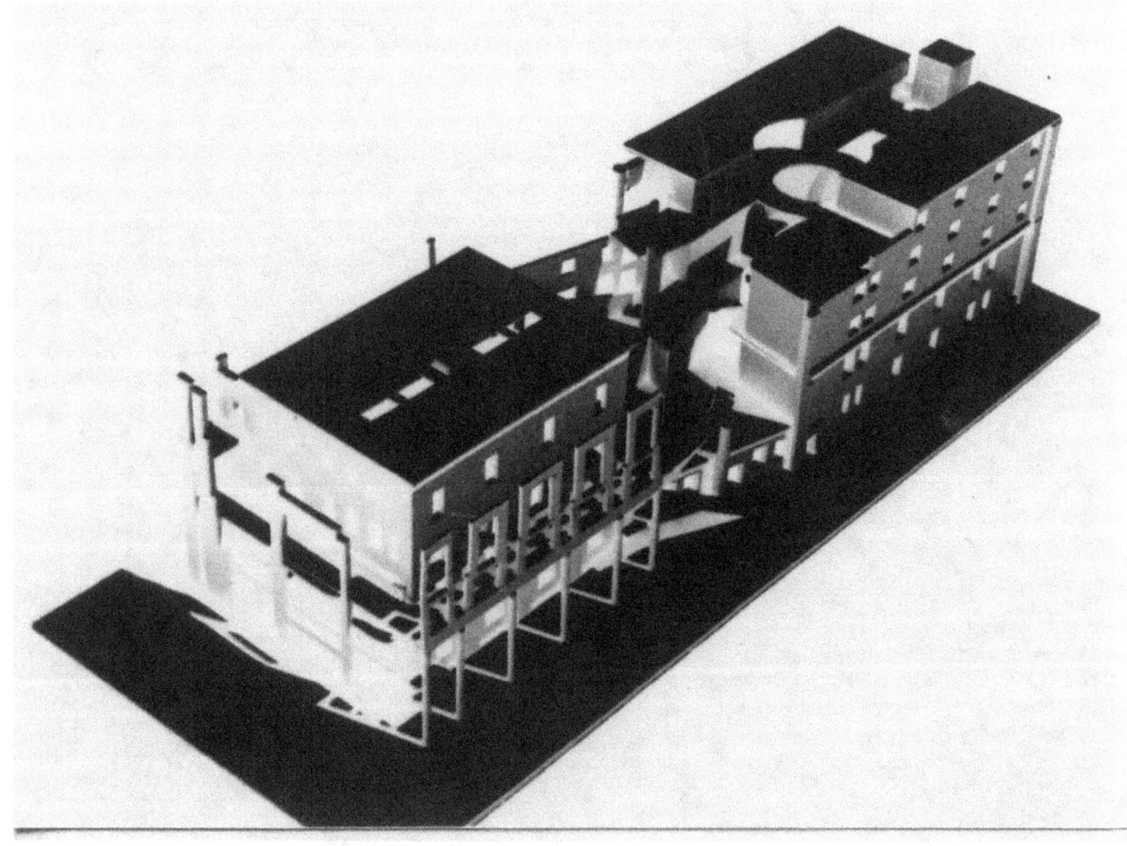

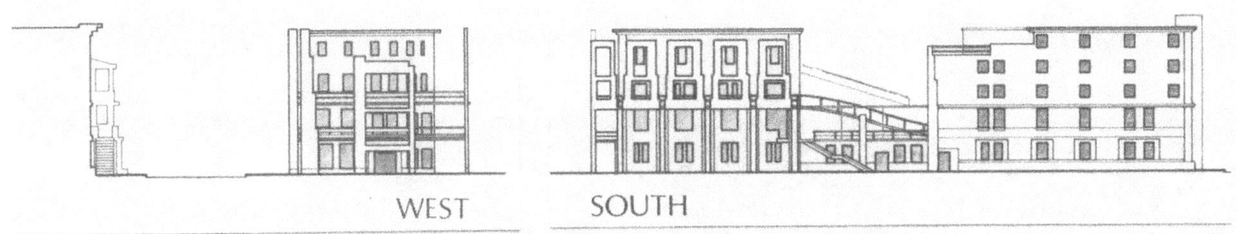
WEST
SOUTH

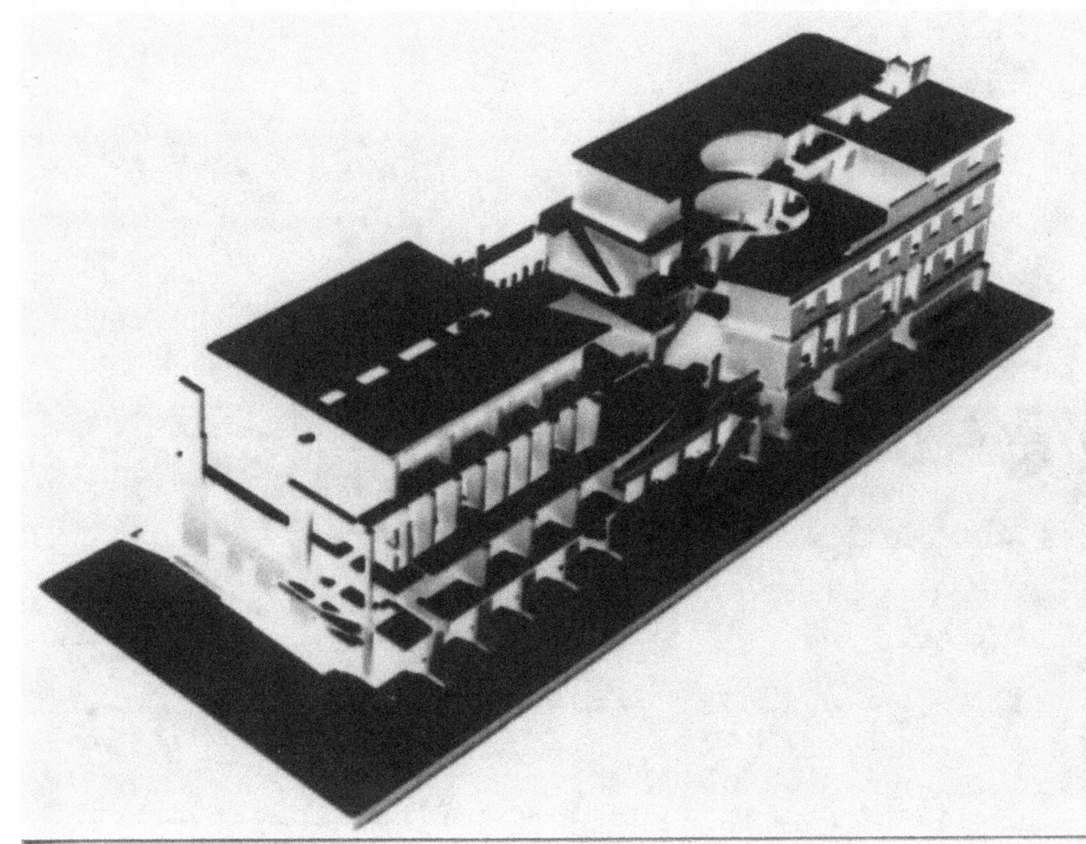

Viking Museum Chicago
Design 6

This project attempts to create a space for the Gokstad, a Viking ship, buried about 1000 years ago, discovered in 1880 and a replica of it sailed to the Chicago World's Fair in 1893. Critical ideas dealt with the siting of the museum, the space for the ship itself and the geographical peculiarities of Norway.
The site is part of the 1893 World's Fair ground and presents approximately where the Gokstad replica landed in 1893. This brought up the idea of arrival but also the action of departure prior to arrival. The leaving of Norway by ship, sailing through a long and narrow fjord was transformed into a building of high walls or canyons that reflect the geography of Norway. The interior was conceived as an anti-climax to the Gokstad ship. A simple space to accentuate an elegant object. To prepare the visitor for this emotional experience he is subjected to spatial extremes by ascending along the blank face of the monumental north wall, turning and entering the actual building only to turn again and participate visually in the long exhibit space for the ship. On the south the building breaks down to a more human scale and relates to the Atlantic, the joint between Europe and America. This act of joining, the sailing of the Gokstad from Norway to Chicago is expressed by placing the museum at the most eastern edge of the site, addressing again the ideas of arrival and departure.

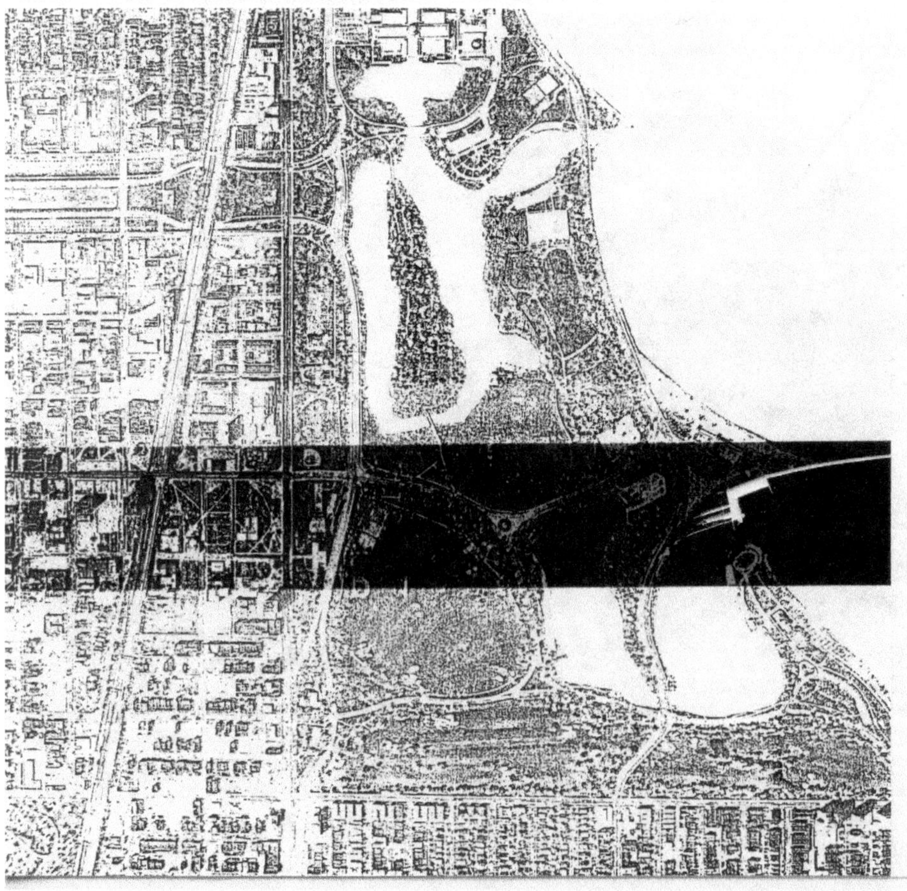

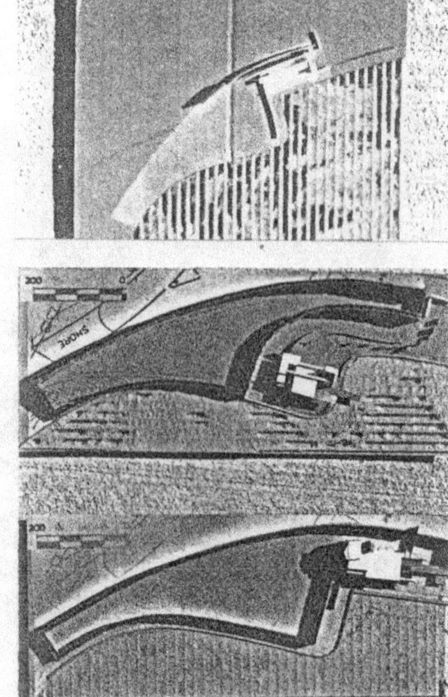

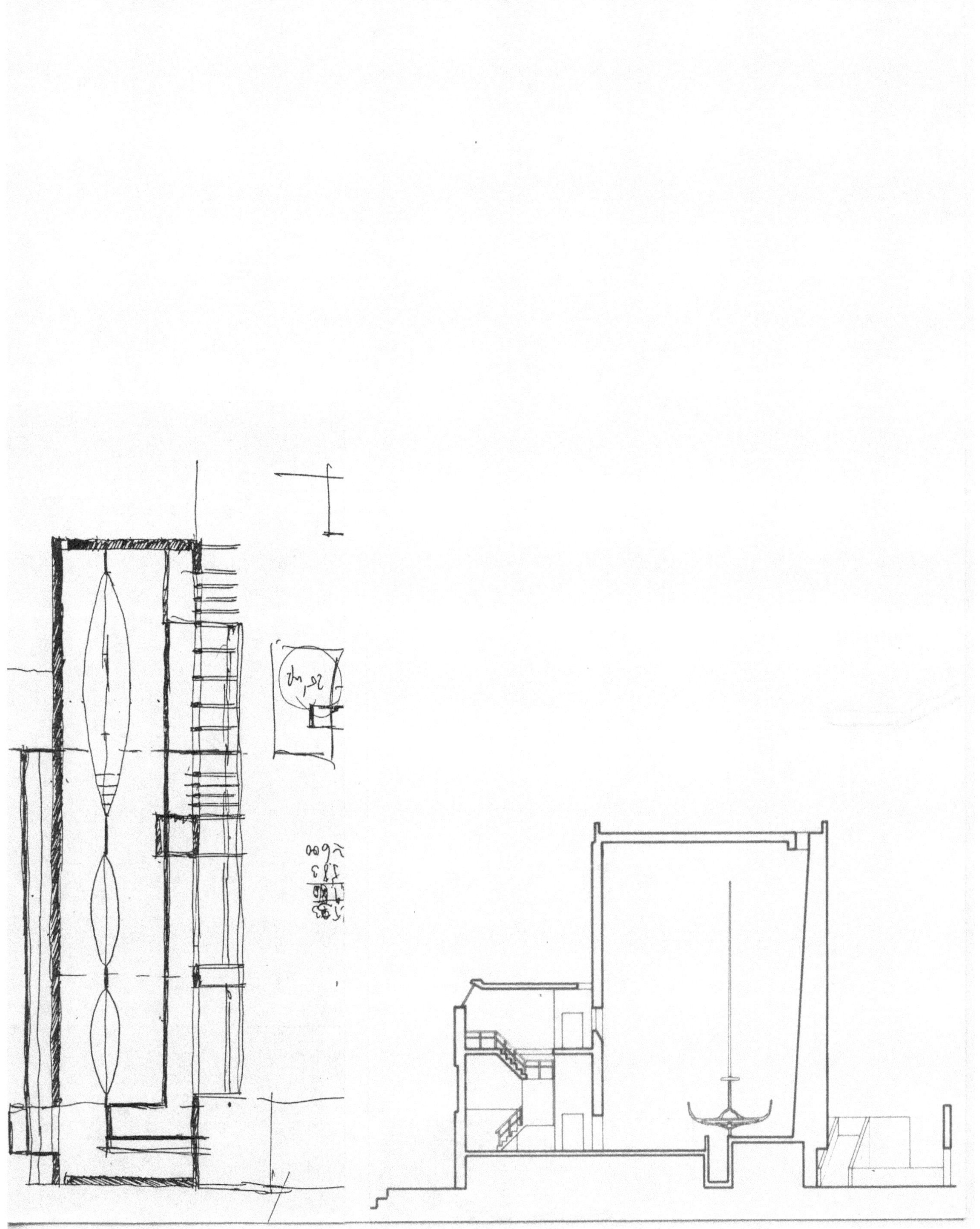

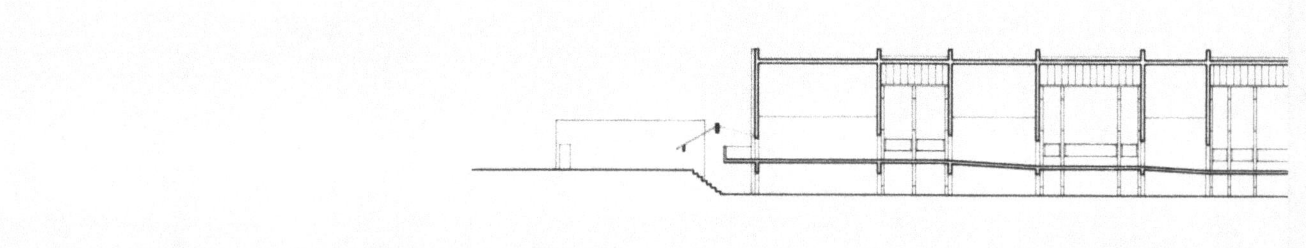

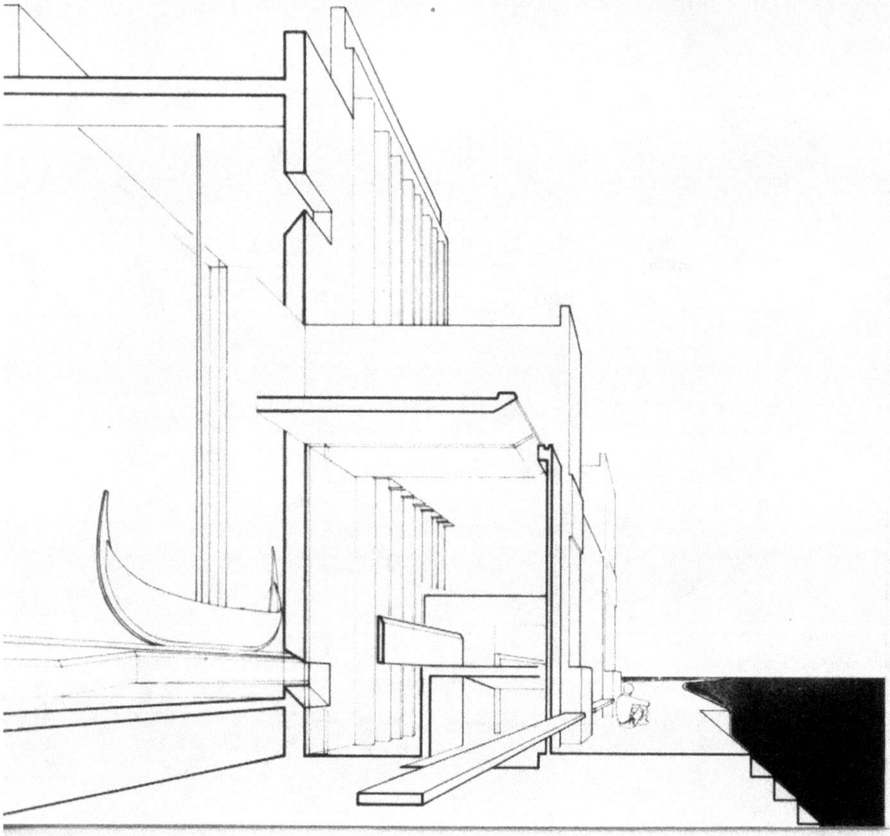

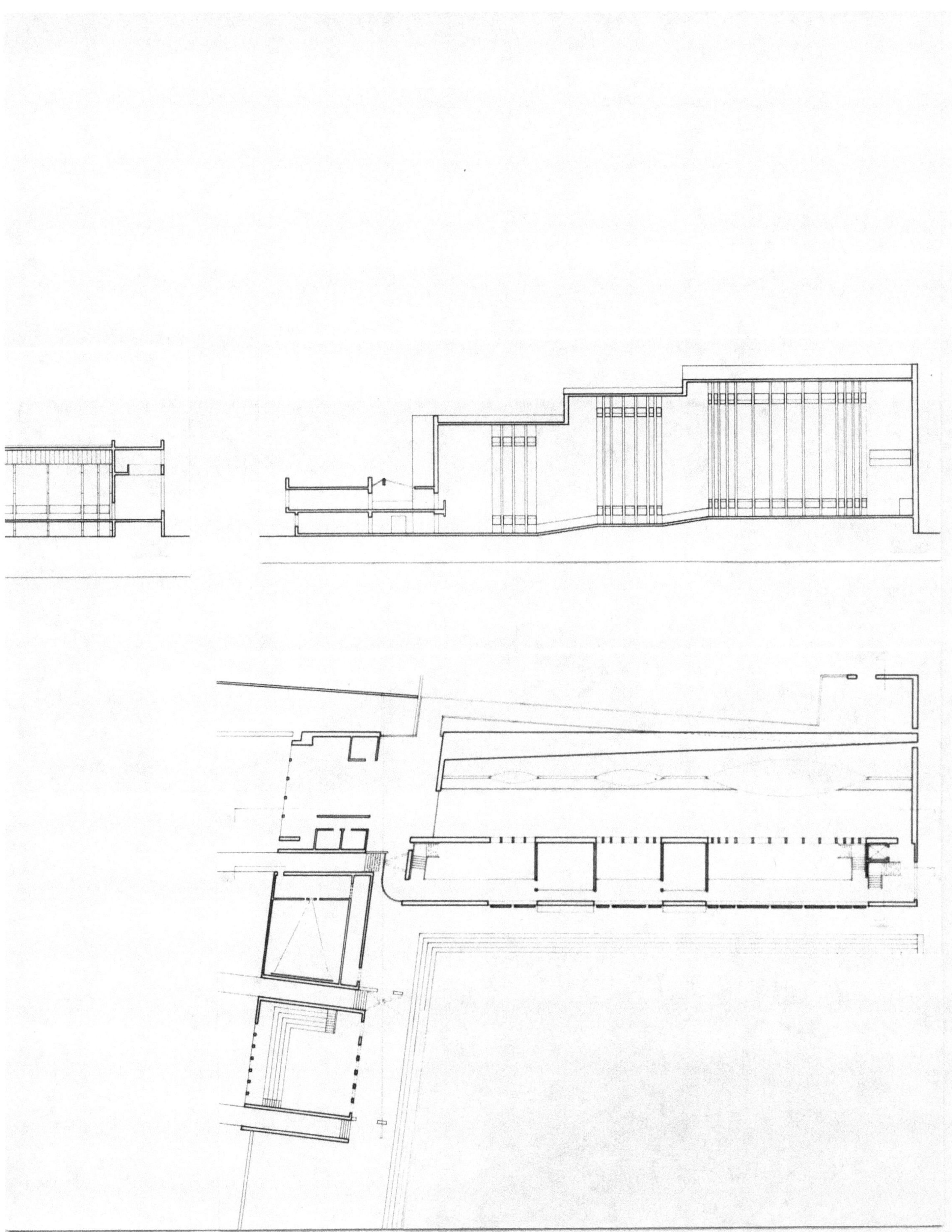

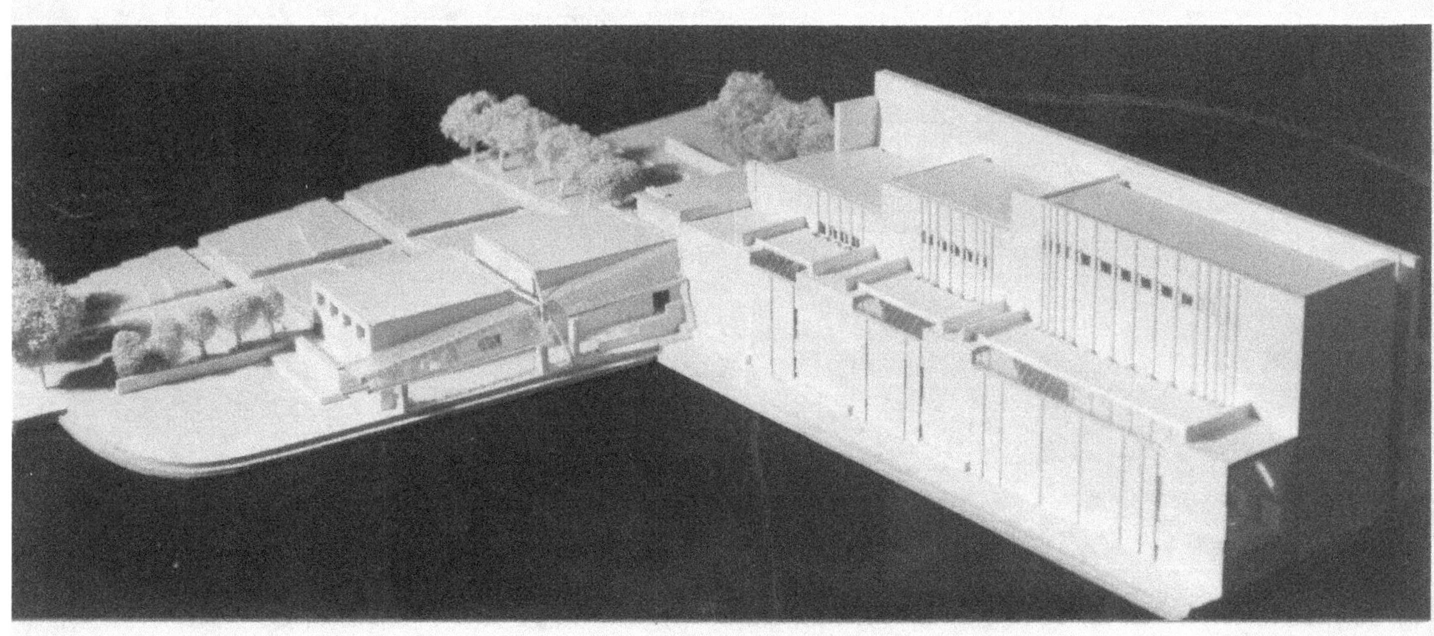

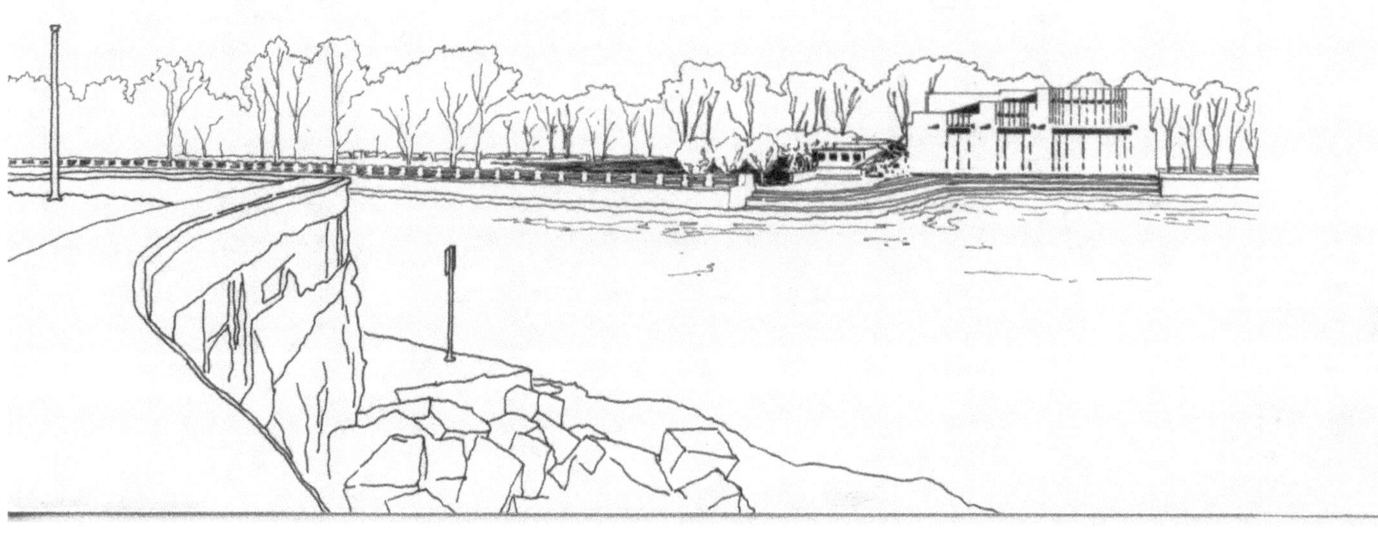

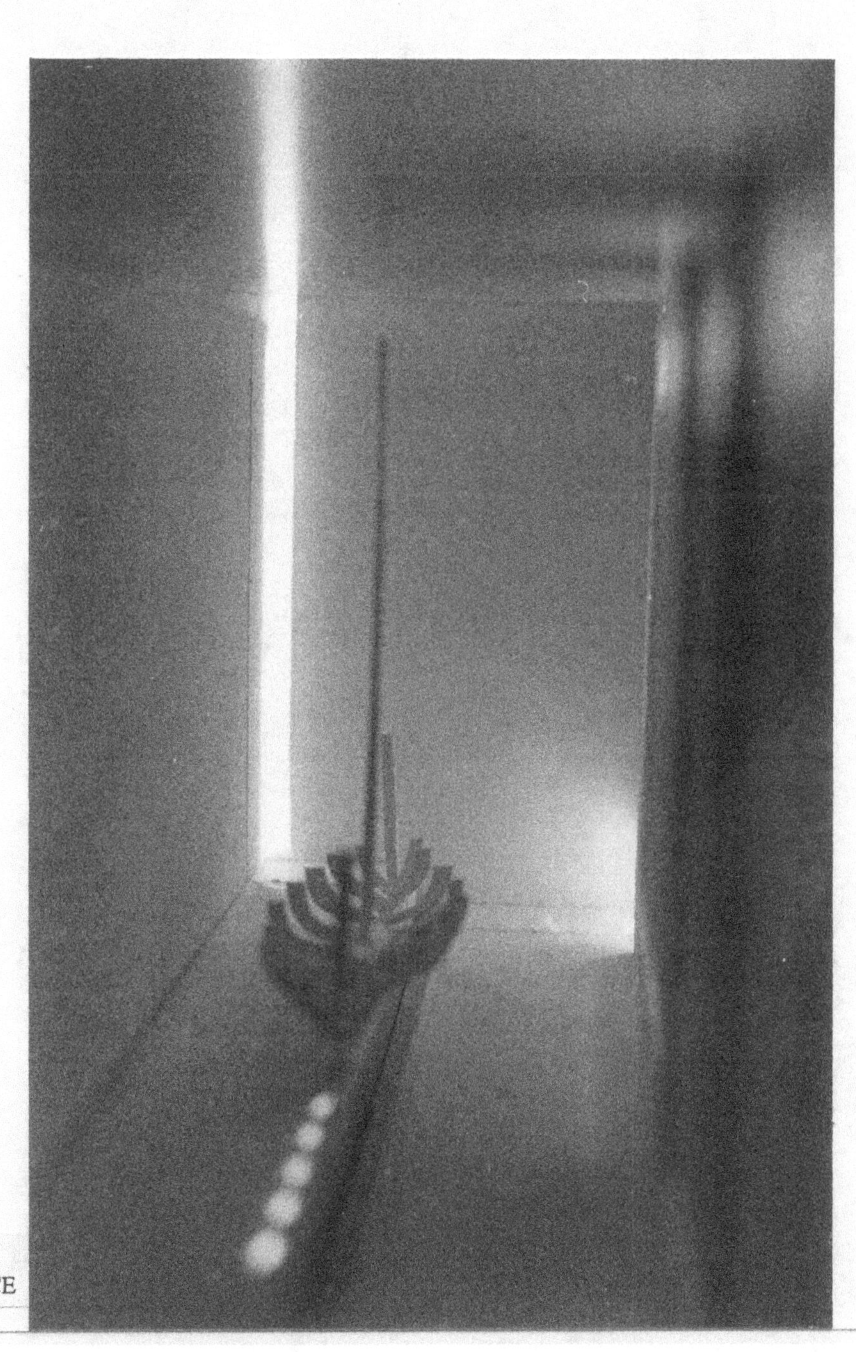

VIEW INTO
EXHIBIT SPACE

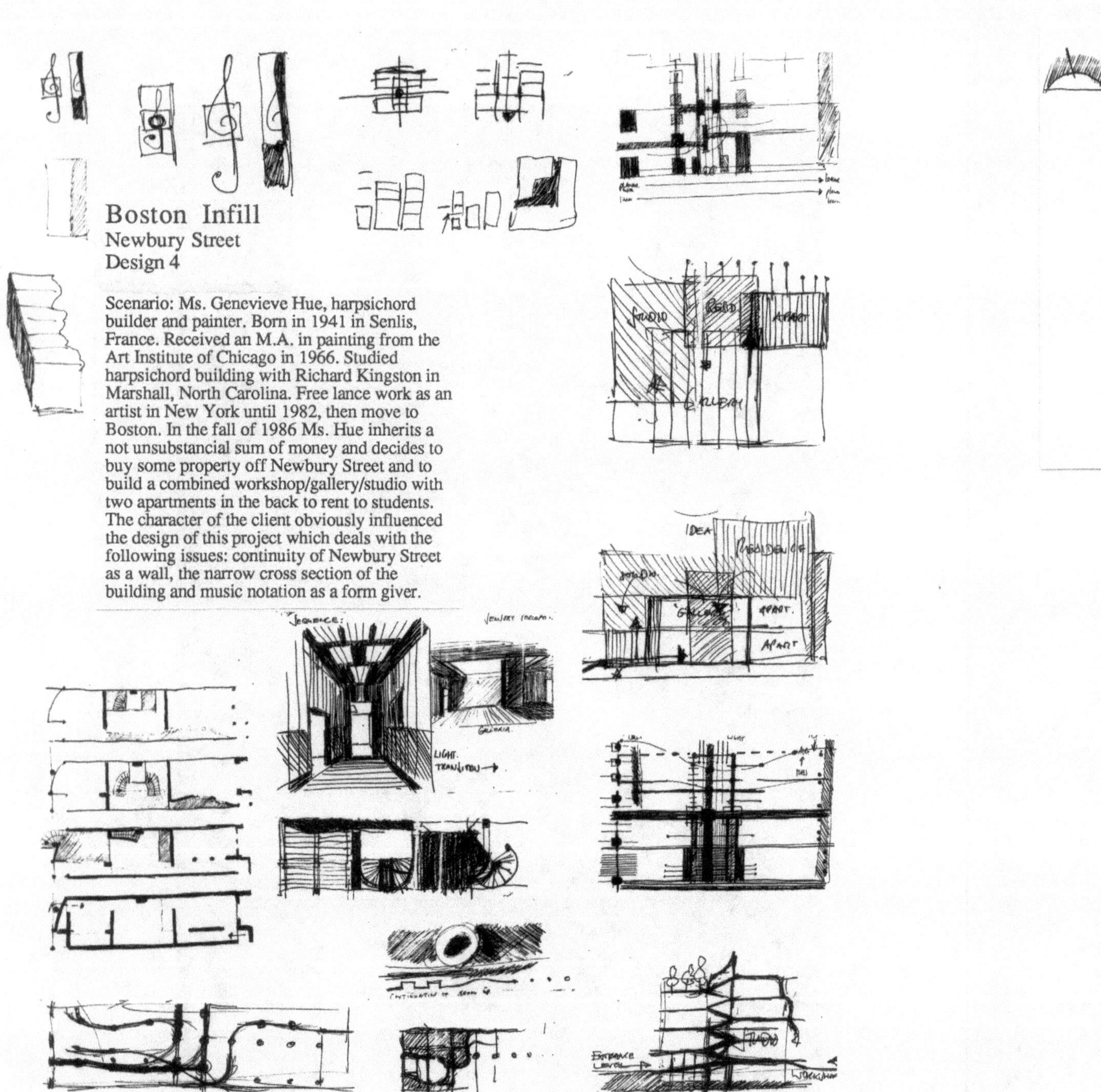

Boston Infill

Newbury Street
Design 4

Scenario: Ms. Genevieve Hue, harpsichord builder and painter. Born in 1941 in Senlis, France. Received an M.A. in painting from the Art Institute of Chicago in 1966. Studied harpsichord building with Richard Kingston in Marshall, North Carolina. Free lance work as an artist in New York until 1982, then move to Boston. In the fall of 1986 Ms. Hue inherits a not unsubstancial sum of money and decides to buy some property off Newbury Street and to build a combined workshop/gallery/studio with two apartments in the back to rent to students. The character of the client obviously influenced the design of this project which deals with the following issues: continuity of Newbury Street as a wall, the narrow cross section of the building and music notation as a form giver.

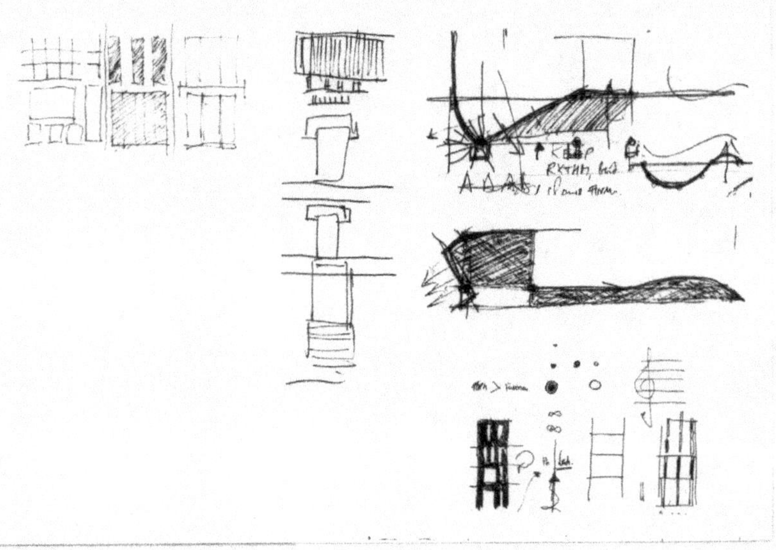

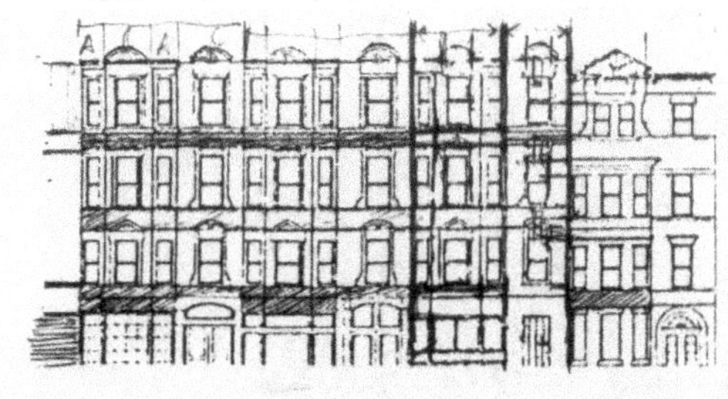

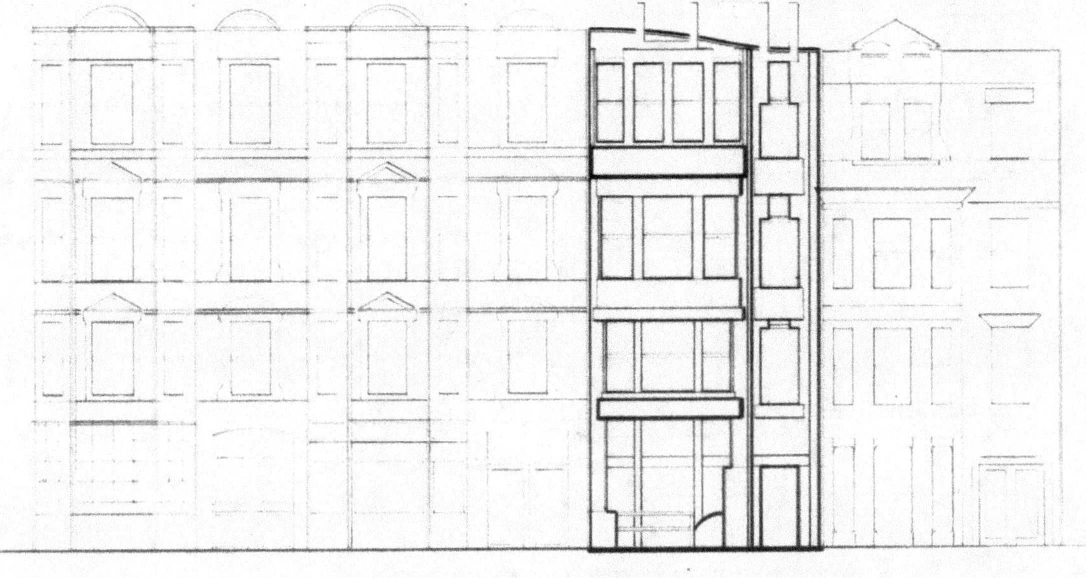

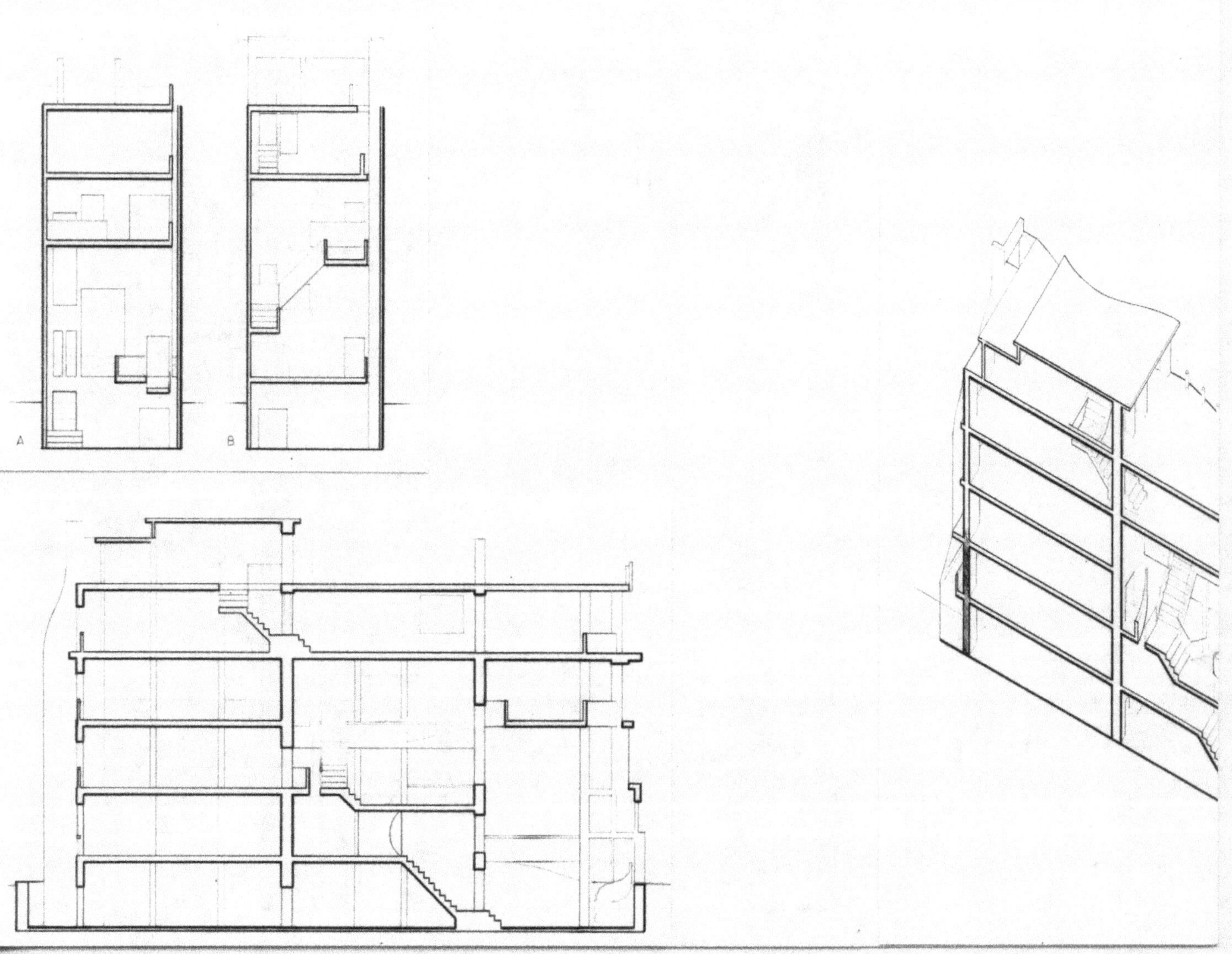
A
B

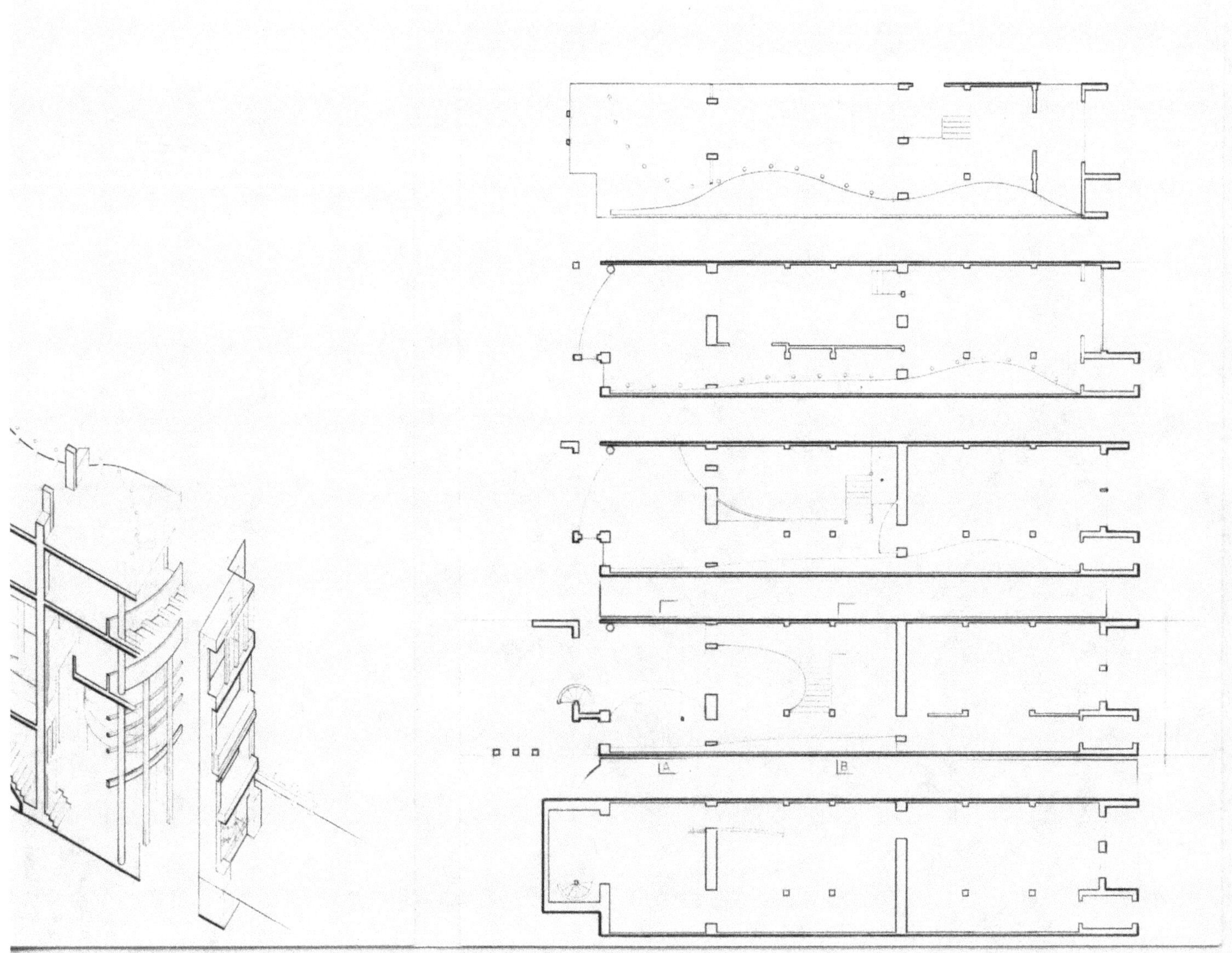

Boston Urban Design and Curley Library

Design 7

Boston is about the absence of history. History in the sense of concealed layers (the german word for history is Geschichte= lit. layering). My design then is about an archeology of Boston where its citizens can reestablish their contact with an-other part of the city. I started by overlaying the existing city with a map from 1794.

Realizing the amount of artificial growth I decided to reverse the development of the land encroaching upon the water by cutting canals which terminate at the old coast line, into the existing fabric. Now the history of the city is more than the two-dimensional red line painted on the sidewalk; it becomes spatial and thus architectural.

In some parts the old coast line turns into buildings that are here not further defined. Another task in the urban design part of this project was to deal with the depression of the interstate artery that cuts the head of Boston in half. My strategy was to link the North End with the Government District, yet let

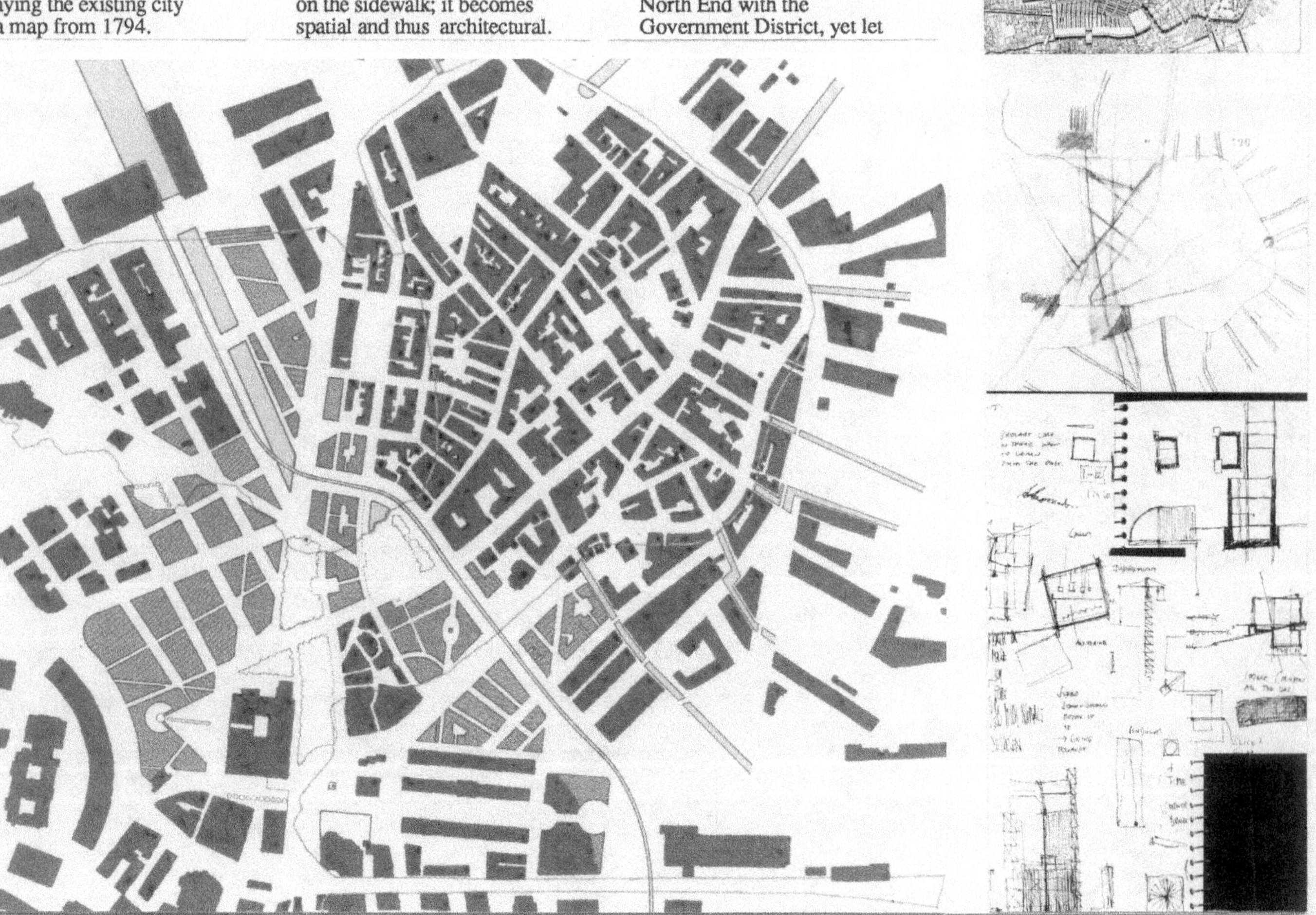

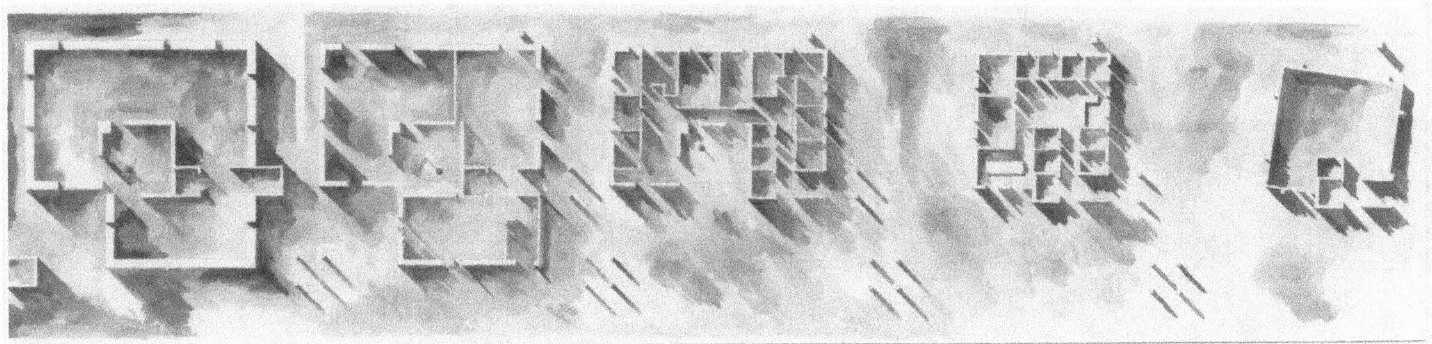

both of them keep their own identity through the insertion of the new Haymarket Square as a buffer in between. This square became also the site for the Curley Research Library.

In the library I am investigating the ideas and implications of time and ambiguity.
This library is a body of knowledge for researchers. Knowledge is aquired over time and is as such always incomplete, i.e. in a state of becoming. This ambiguity between becoming and being is expressed in the siting of the building. There is a dry moat surrounding the library, exposing the ancient layers in the ground, making entry possible only via a bridge that, when the library is closed, folds back and becomes part of the wall.

The program for the library also suggests a schism in that the largest part of the library is not accessible to the general public but only to researchers. Only the auditorium/gallery and the Curley Memorial Room can be entered by the public.
The two basement levels appropriately house the reserved stacks, the forbidden part of the library, the underground past, simultaneously exposed and hidden, accessible only by special permission. The open stacks share the two floors above ground level together with the entry piece and the Curley Memorial Room. The shifted cube above the open stacks is the reading room, one large volume whose edge is eaten away by the central vertical pendulum space which shows the reading room's dependency or for that matter everything's dependency on time. The tilted and shifted gallery/auditorium at the top of the library symbolize the current state of confusion and instability in the body of knowledge.
The truss houses the elevator, a tentative link. Towering above everything else is the crane, symbol of change in every city.

row of tall buildings
grey sky with thin trusses;
cranes
that don't fly anymore

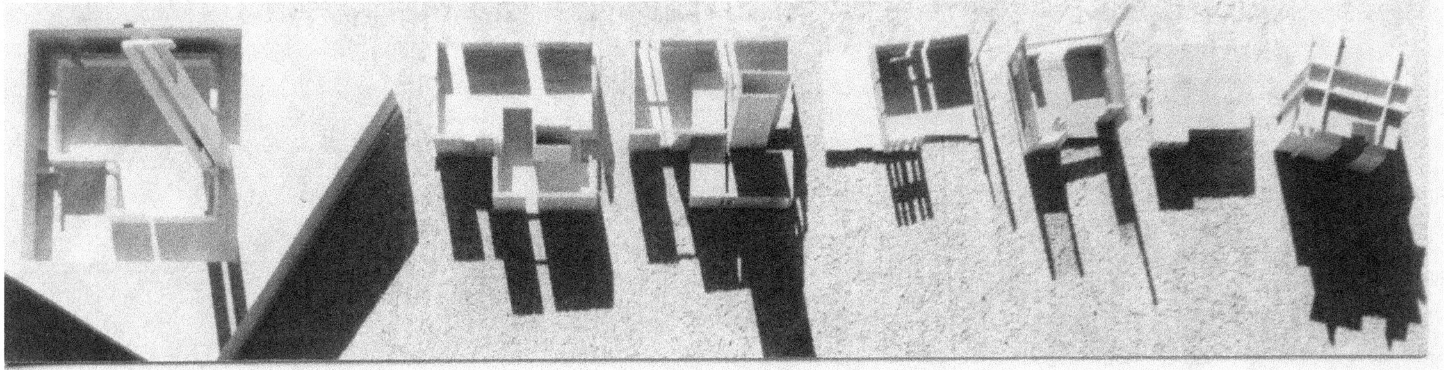

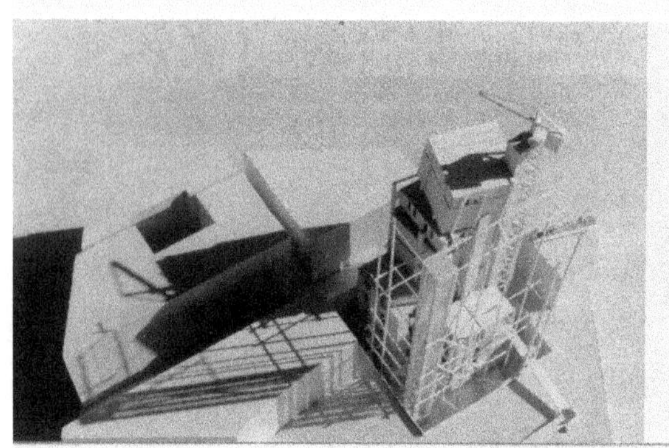

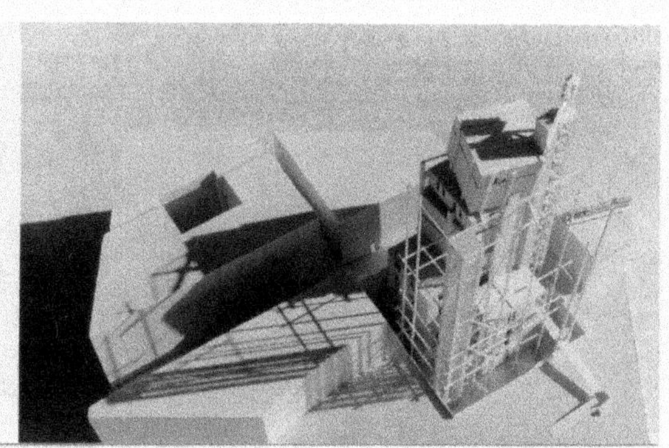

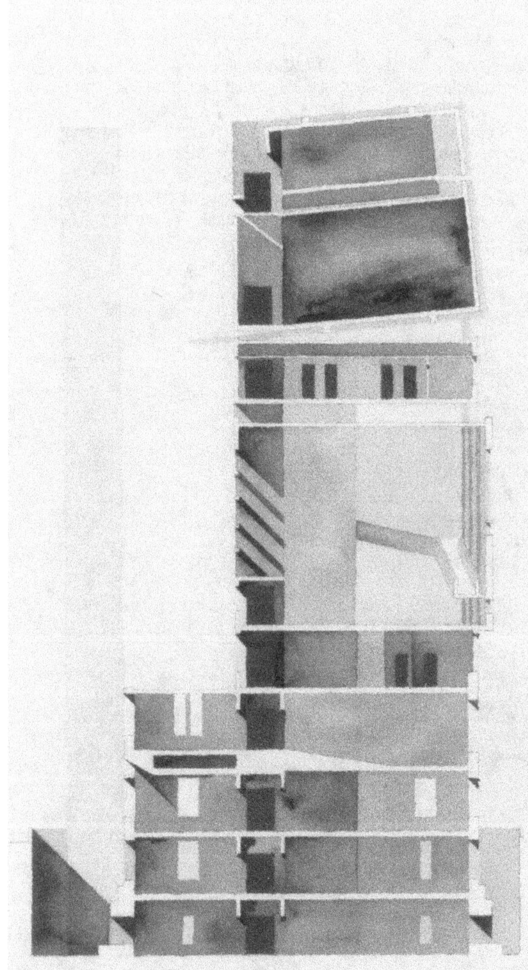

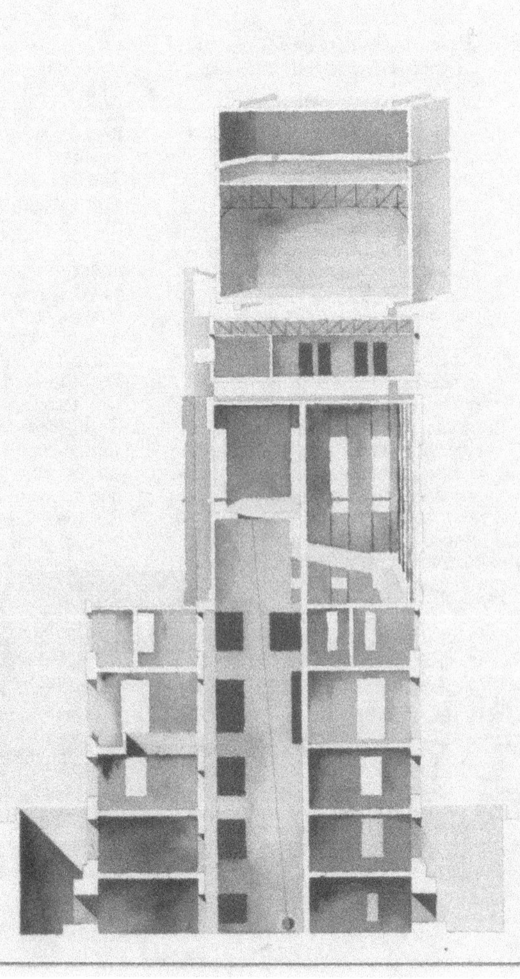

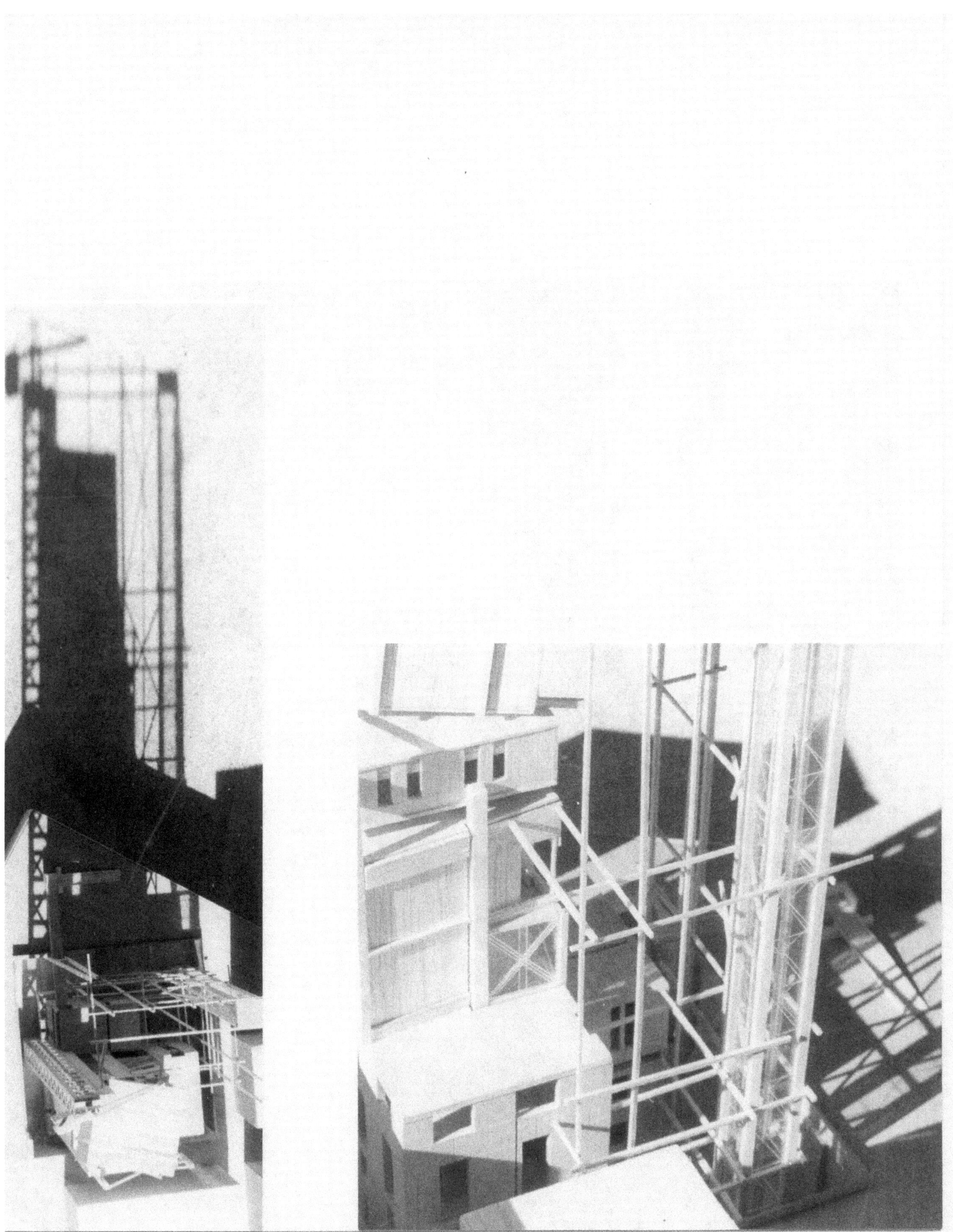

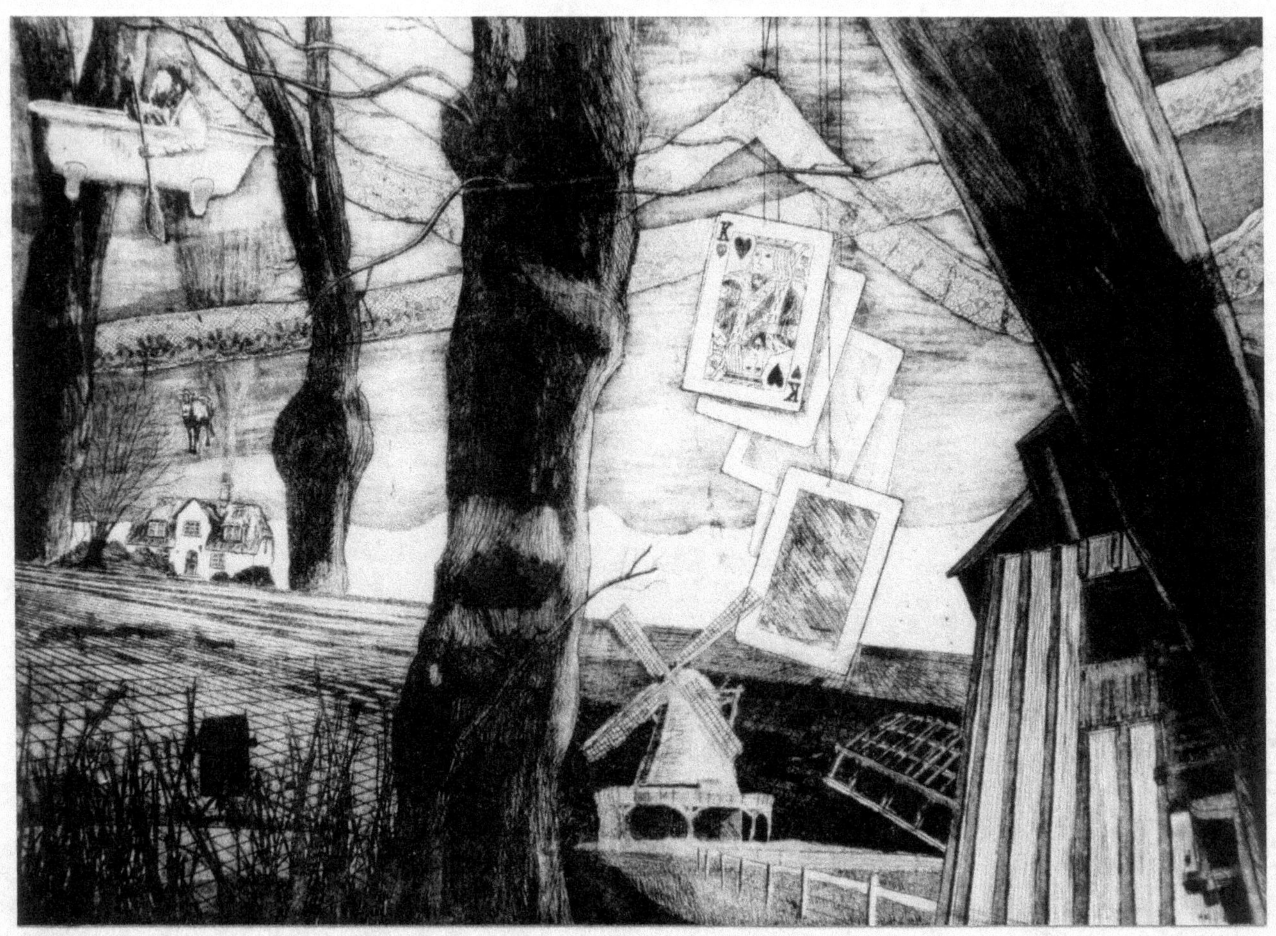

'DUKE OF CLUBS'
ETCHING AND AQUATINT ON COPPER PLATE
SUMMER 1988

PHOTOGRAPH
VENICE, ITALY
SUMMER 1988

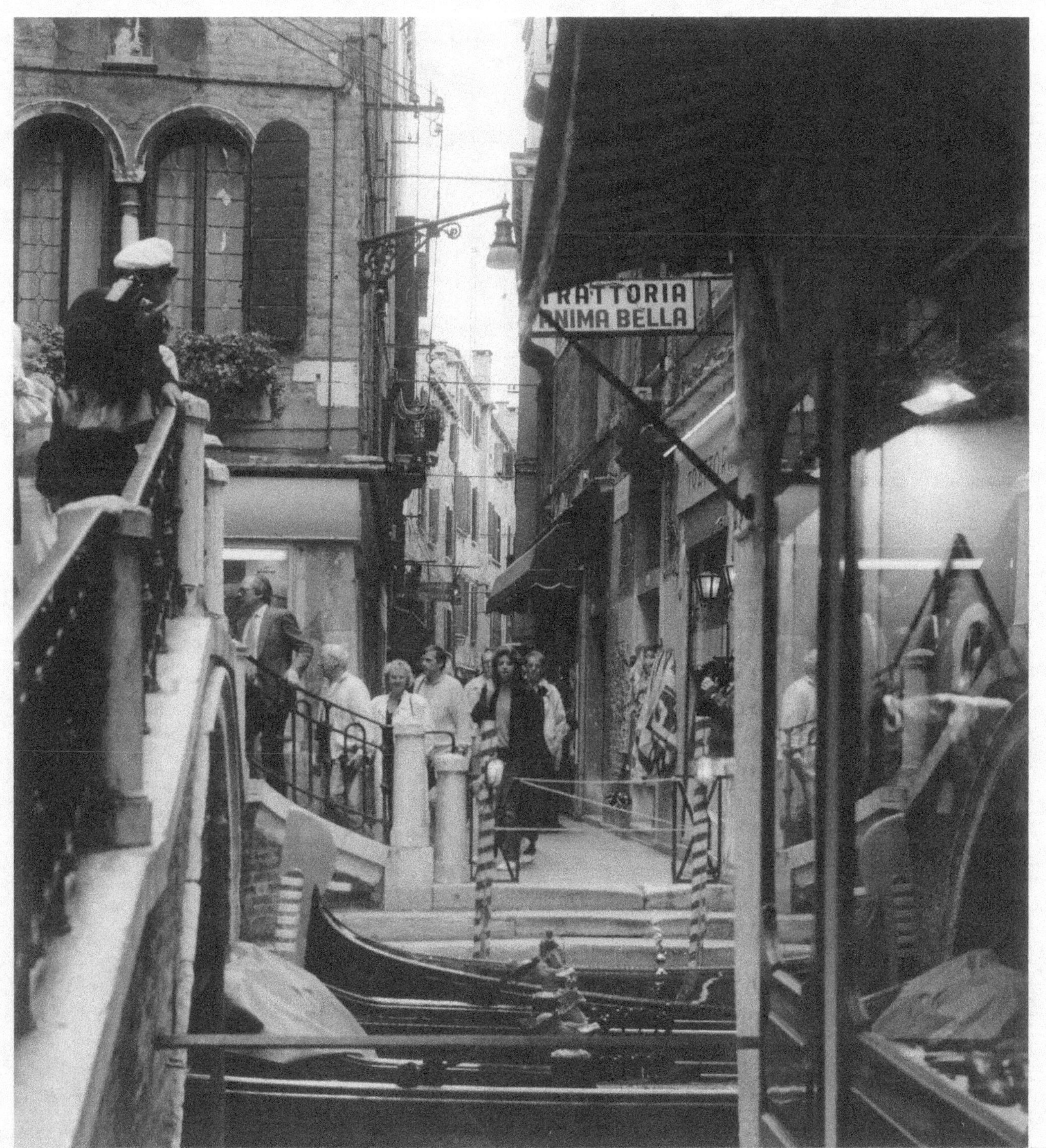
TRATTORIA
ANIMA BELLA

Facsimile of Photocopy of Original

Greyscale values disappear and contrast is increased. Crude and also effective. The spiral binding holes are still visible in the gutter.

1986	SUMMER	1+2
1986	FALL	3
1987	SPRING	4
1987	FALL	5
1988	SPRING	6
1988	FALL	7
1989	SPRING	8

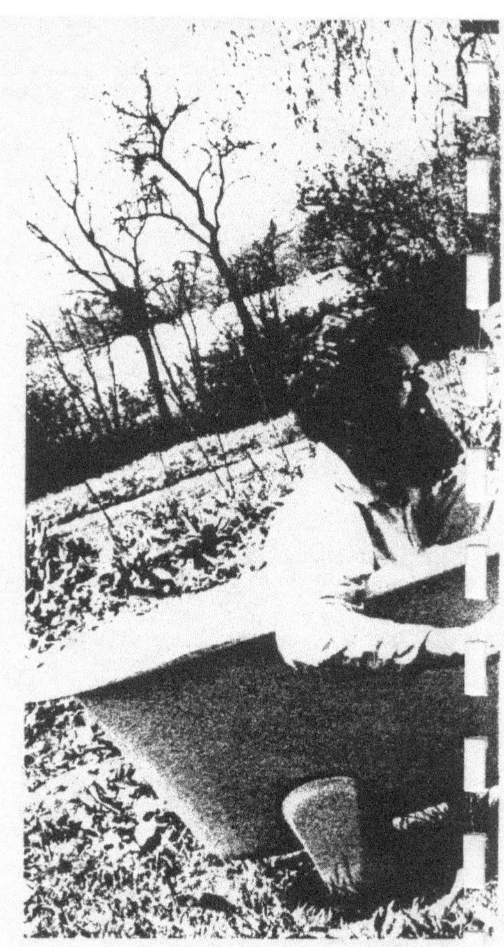

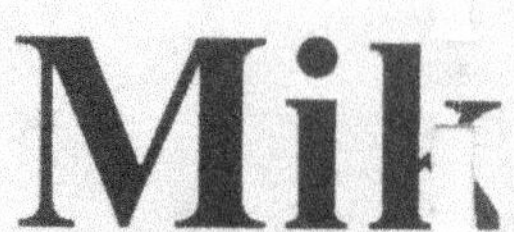

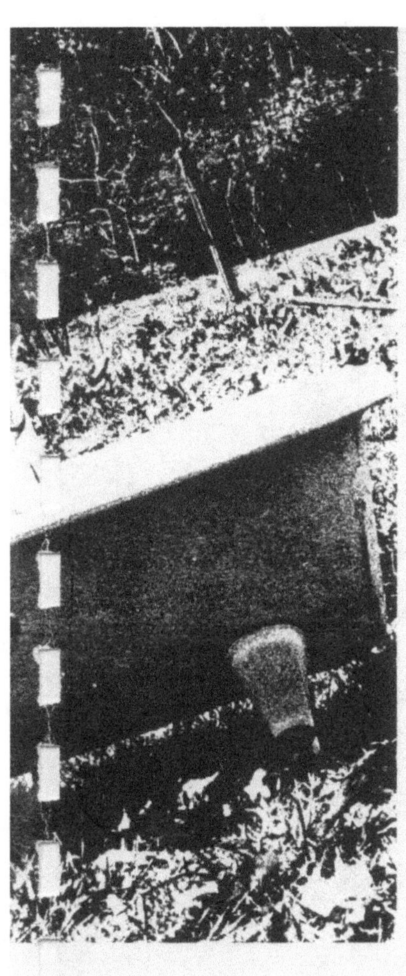

esch'

1986-1989
undergraduate work

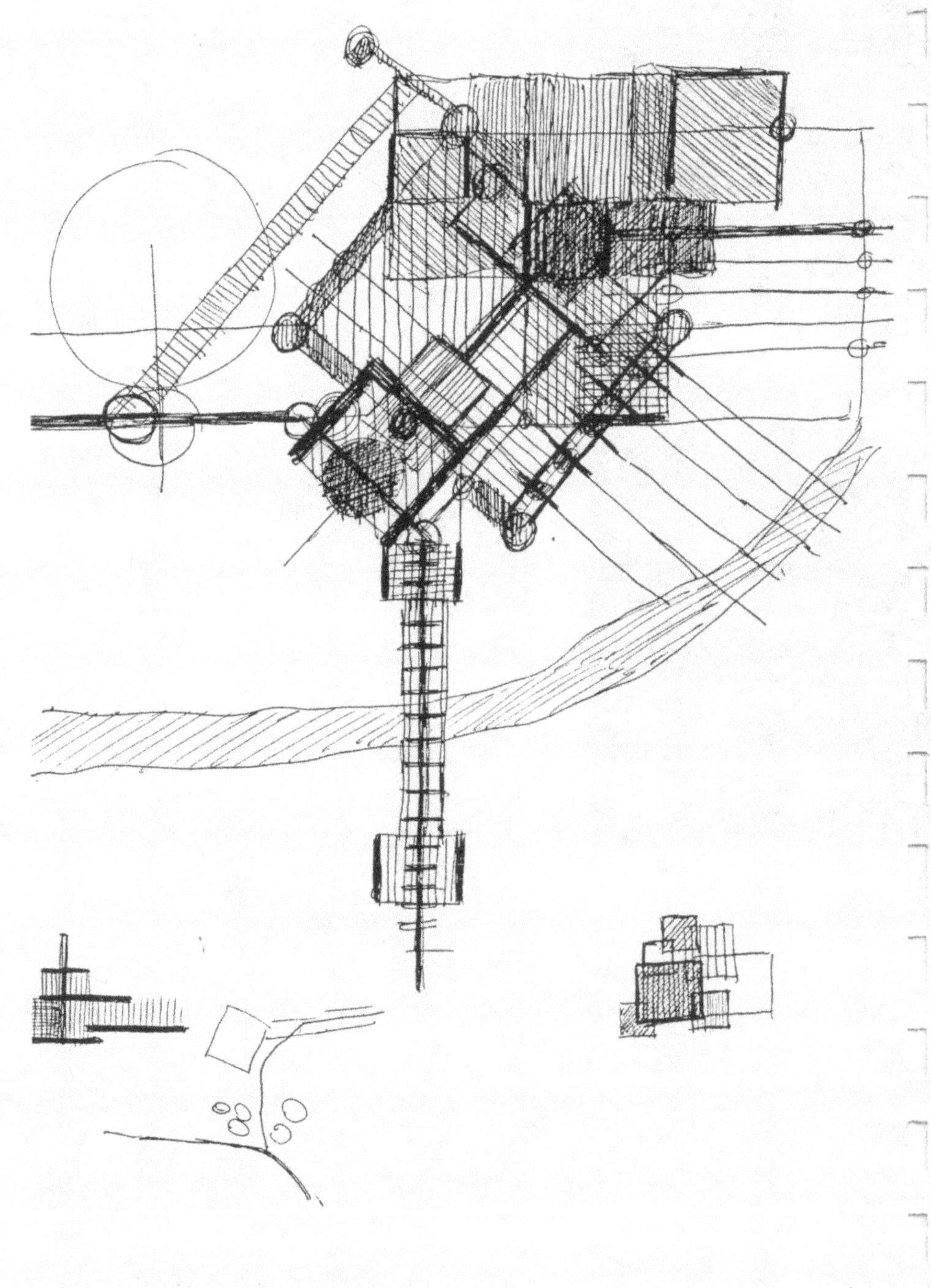

1986

Gate House

Addirondack Mountains,
New York
Design 3

The gate house creates an entry to a villa on the other side of the bridge. This villa was built by Adolf Loos. Thus I appropriated Loos' ideas on architecture for the design of the gate house. The major characteristics include the following: carved space, design from inside out, and Raumplan, a name coined by Loos for his 'space-plan' design, i.e. interrelated but differentiated spaces.
The building itself is conceived as a frame with a massive central core which marks the turning point of the approach. This shift in direction also indicates a horizontal change from public to private functions. The building displays a 'closed' face towards the public access side (roadway with bridge) and opens up in the more private part towards nature.

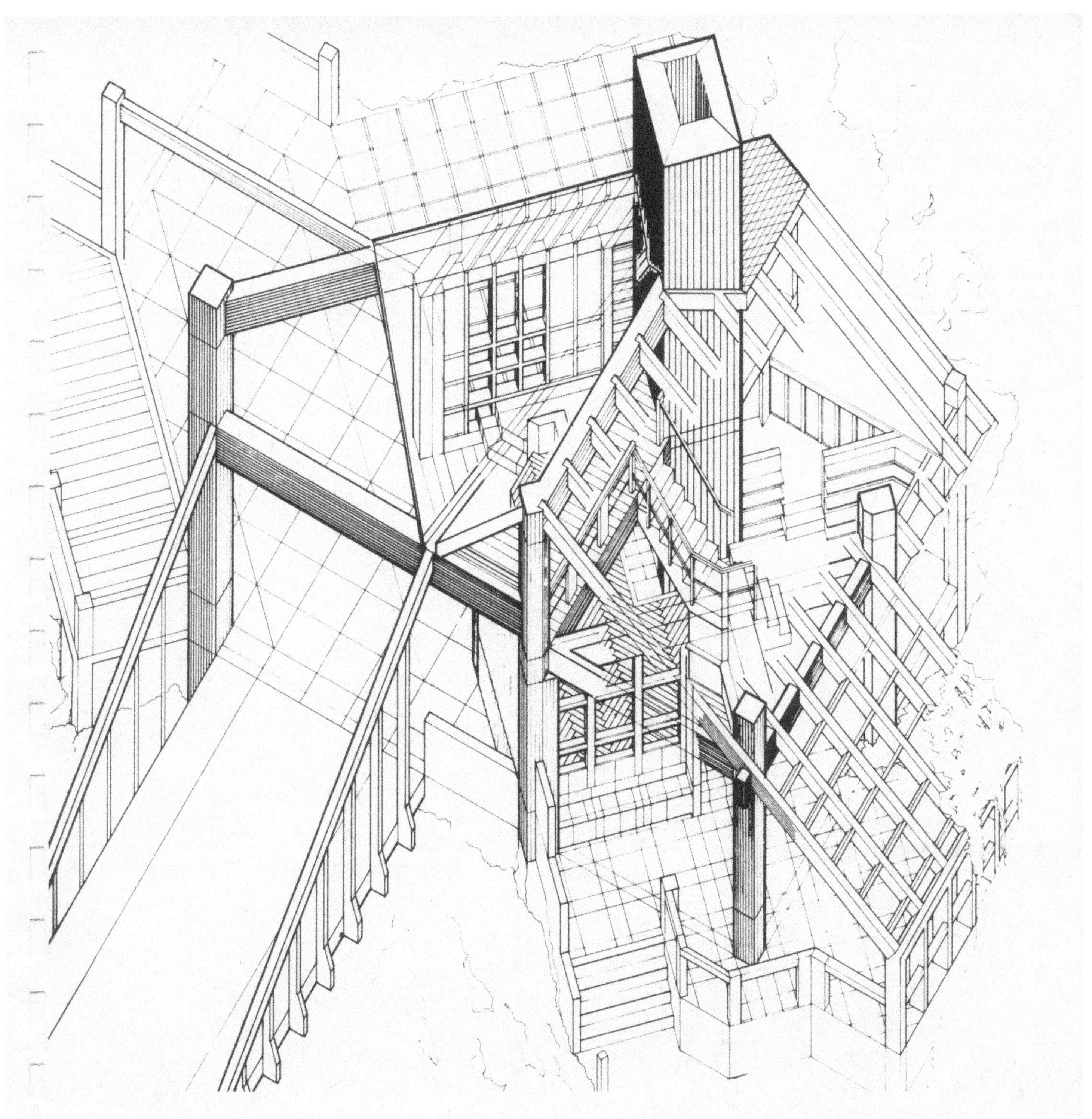

Monument to Commemoration and Condemnation

Design 4

1987

Deconstructivism as theory base.

"Deconstruction is not a method, but a form of consciousness to some object."

Commemoration:
to serve as a memento or reminder; to honor the memory of by some observance or celebration.

Condemnation:
to pronounce adverse judgement on; to declare incurable.

Both ideas for this monument address thought or memory, and both can be viewed as intangible qualities. Thus the monument can not be occupied physically but only mentally. It can not be built, hence it is not a monument. Yet it can exist as a sign which refers to the real thing. Two deconstructed cubes, one in the ground, the other above ground, separated by a glass plate that allows visual access but prevents concrete experience.

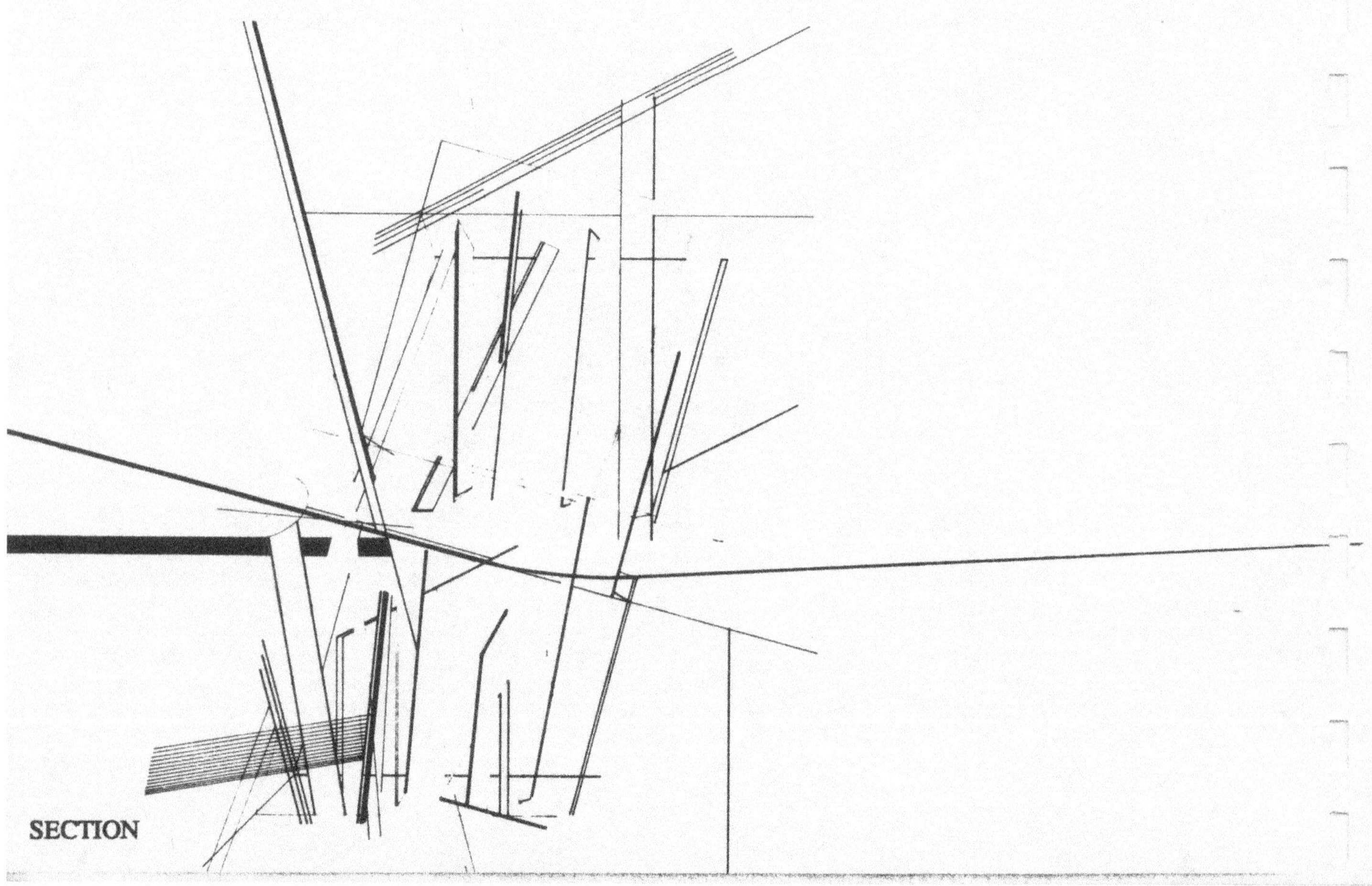

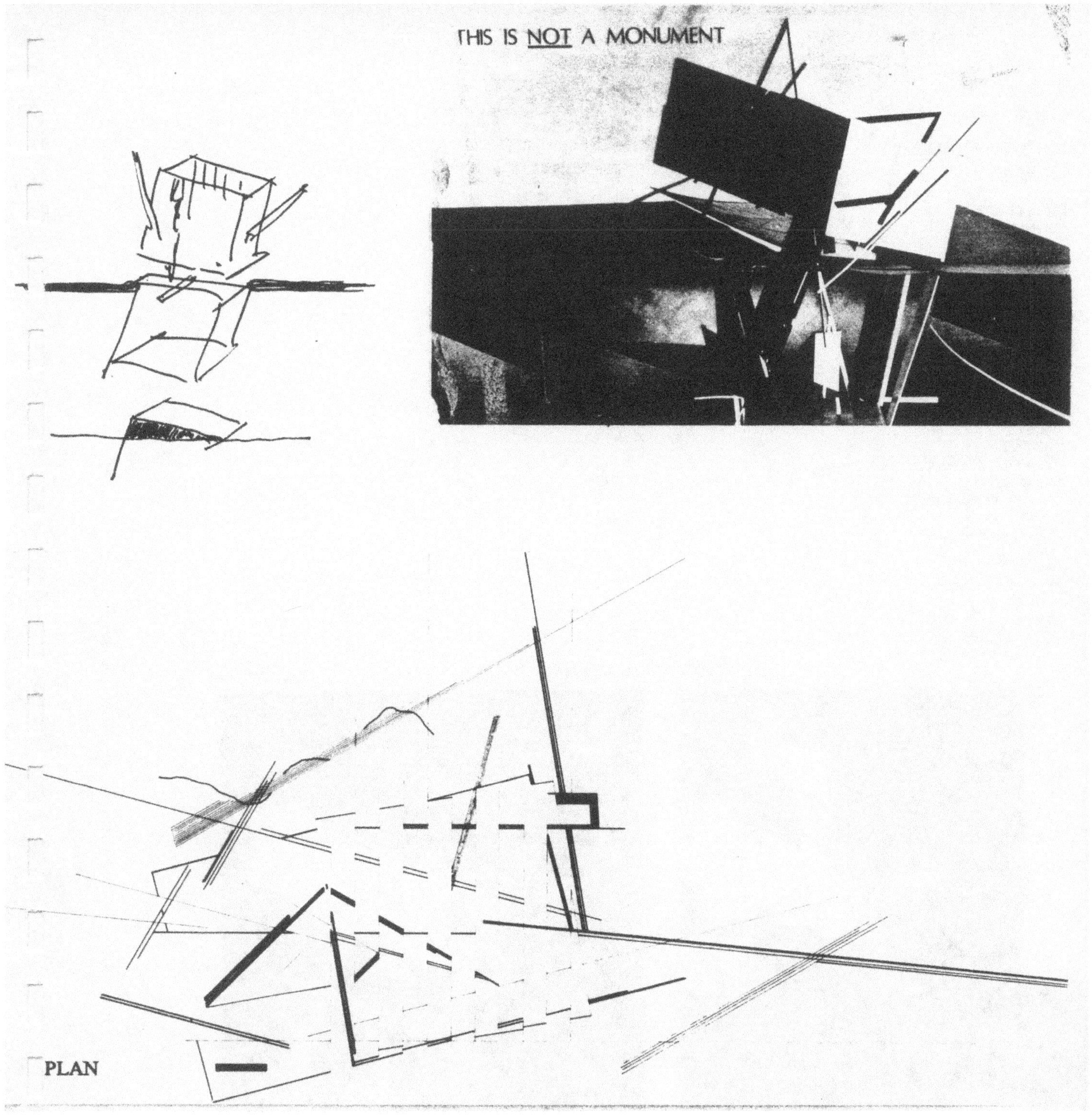
THIS IS NOT A MONUMENT
PLAN

Tower for Observation and Contemplation
Design 4

1987

Project Parts:
1. Rolling hills.
2. Tower with
3. Observation space,
4. Meditation space,
and
5. Path that connects both spaces.

Ideas:
tower
vertical,
to observe,
look into outside world.
to meditate,
look into inside world.
duality,
expansion of space
light
open
contraction of space
dark
closed.

For this project I studied the theory base of De Stijl which originated in the Netherlands. Subsequently I decided to investigate the idea of tower in terms of the DeStijl theory but also in concrete terms as a windmill. The two distinct spaces became two elevator boxes connected with a steel cable. If the observation space moves up the meditation space moves down and vice versa. The whole building can be turned to allow for viewing in all directions. In order to escape the dilemma of a purely orthogonal architecture the exit out of the tower is managed via an s-shaped slide.

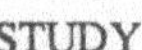

STUDY MODELS

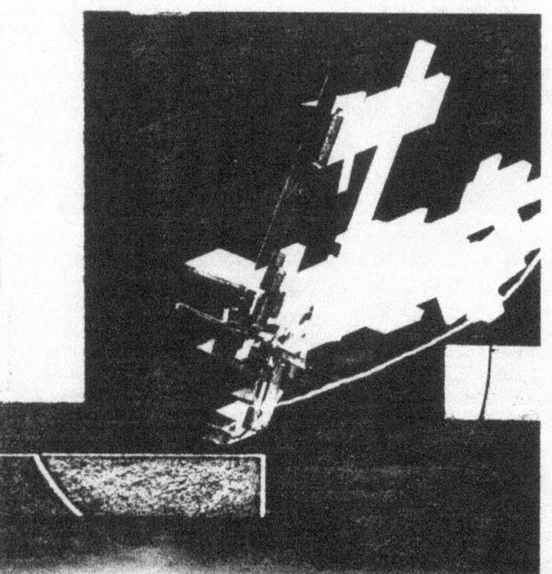

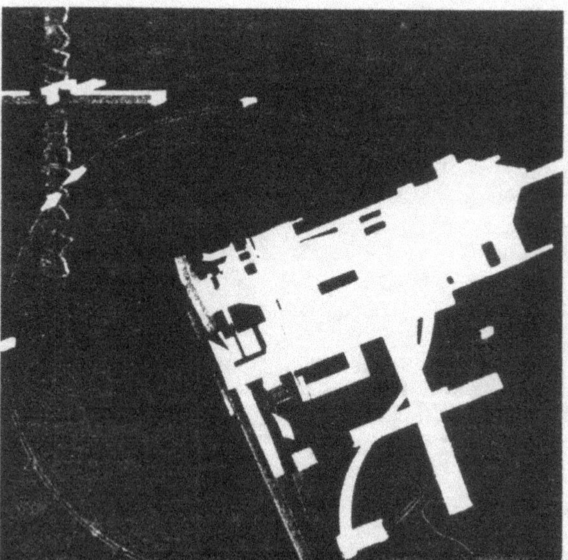

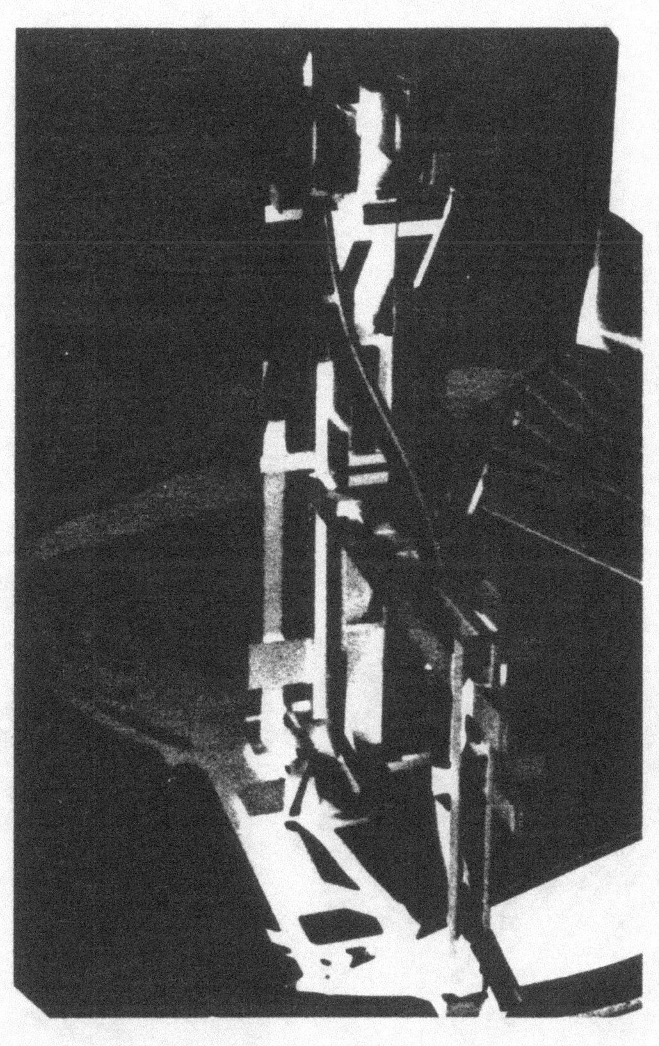
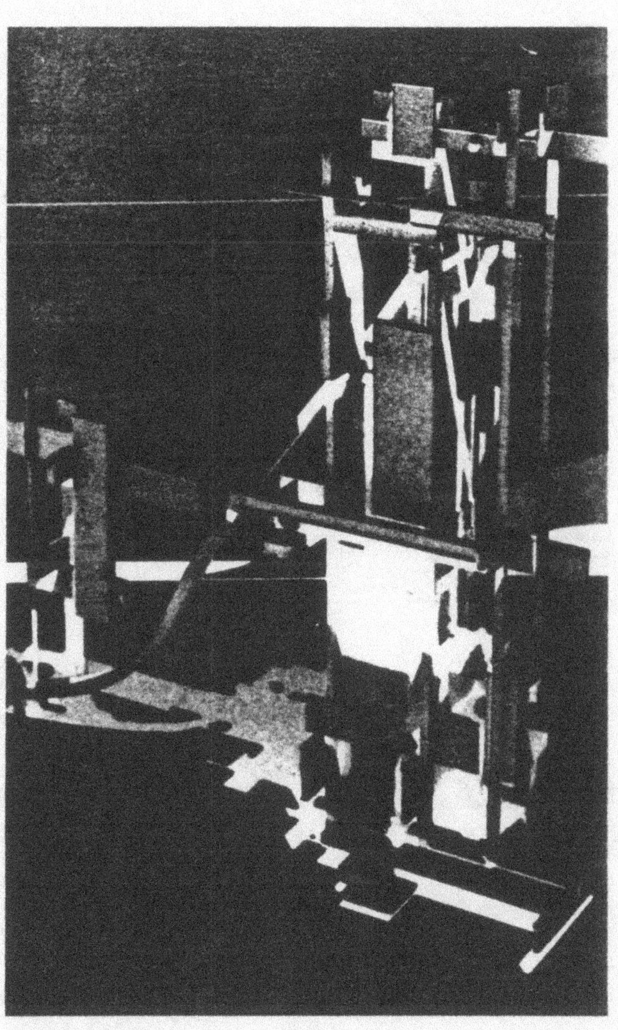
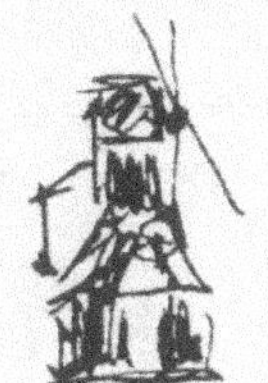
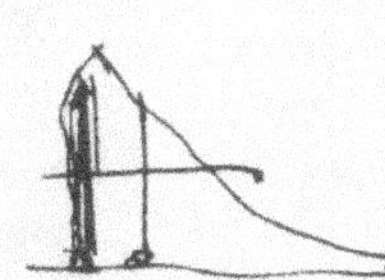
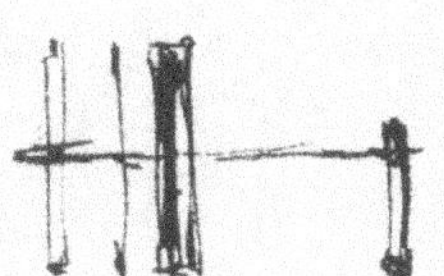
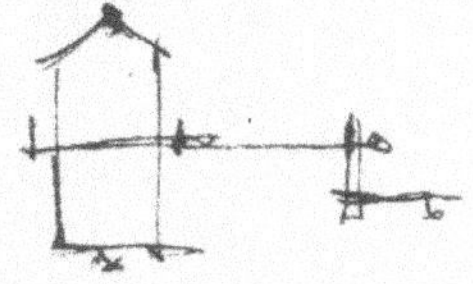

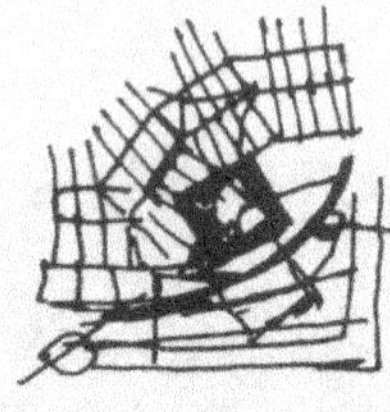

Center for Latin-American Scholars

Lake Alice, Gainesville
Design 3

1986

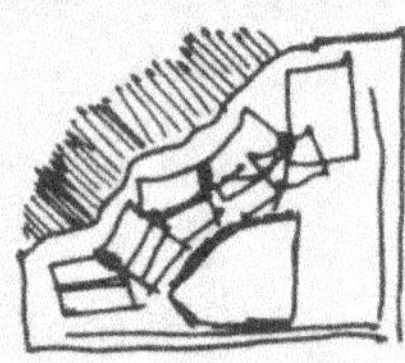

At one scale the building complex creates a joint between Lake Alice and Museum Road. At another scale the central courtyard joins the two major programmes: private apartments which grow finger-like into the lake and public activities (auditorium, offices) which are adjacent to the more public realm, the street. The whole building complex becomes the meeting ground between nature and man-made nature while the courtyard creates a meeting place for different cultures. Even the layout for the individual apartments reflects on the micro scale the concept of joint and center. Here the stairs create a joint between the different spaces in the apartment.

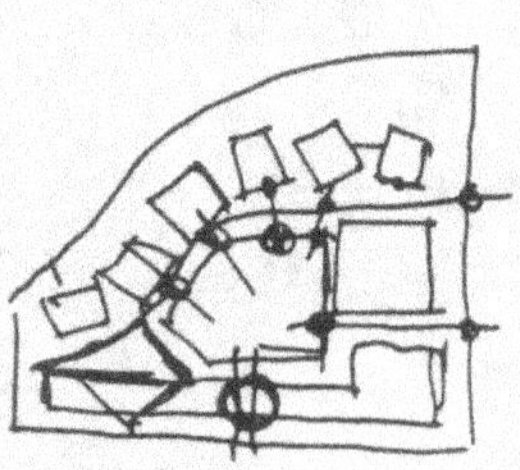

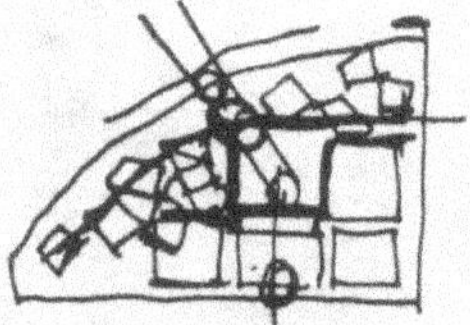

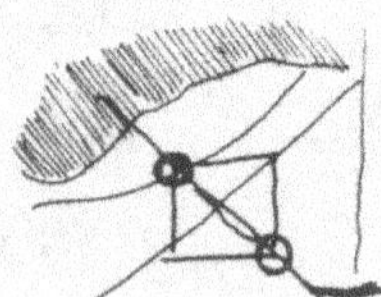

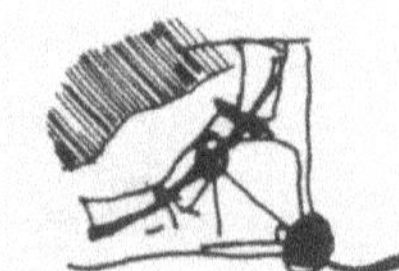

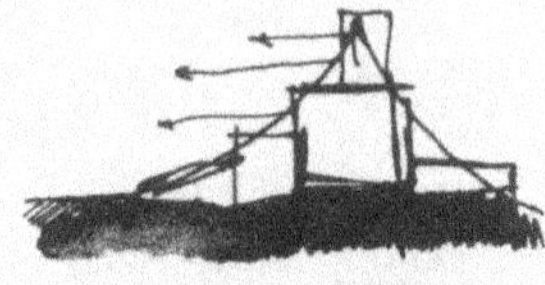

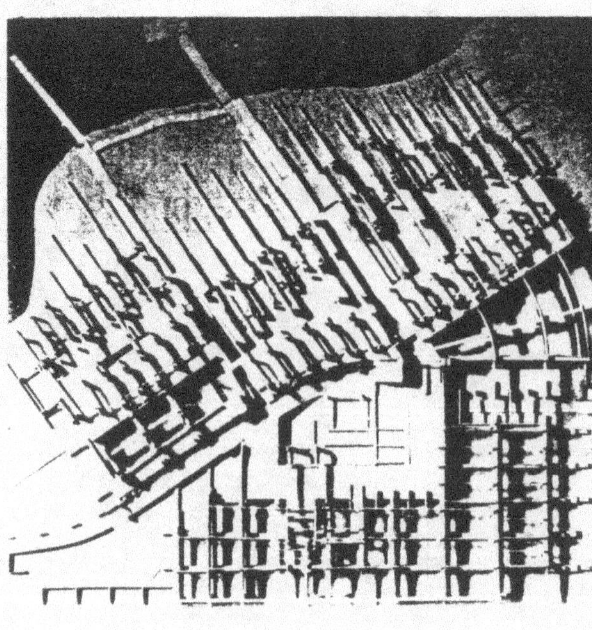

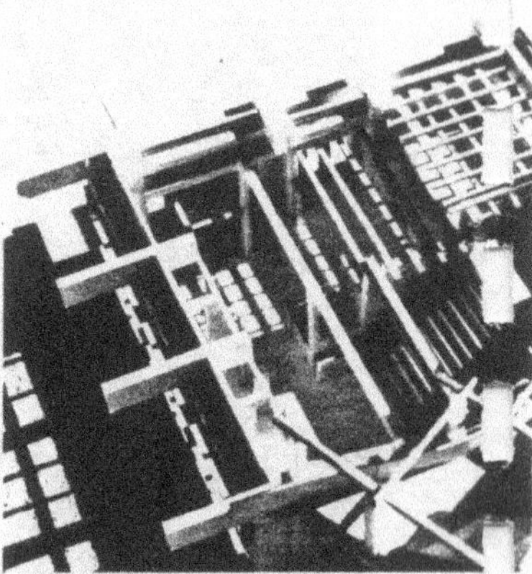

CENTRAL

COURTYARD

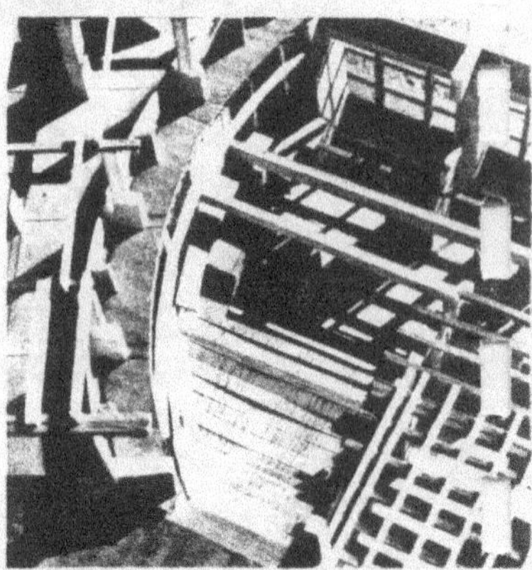

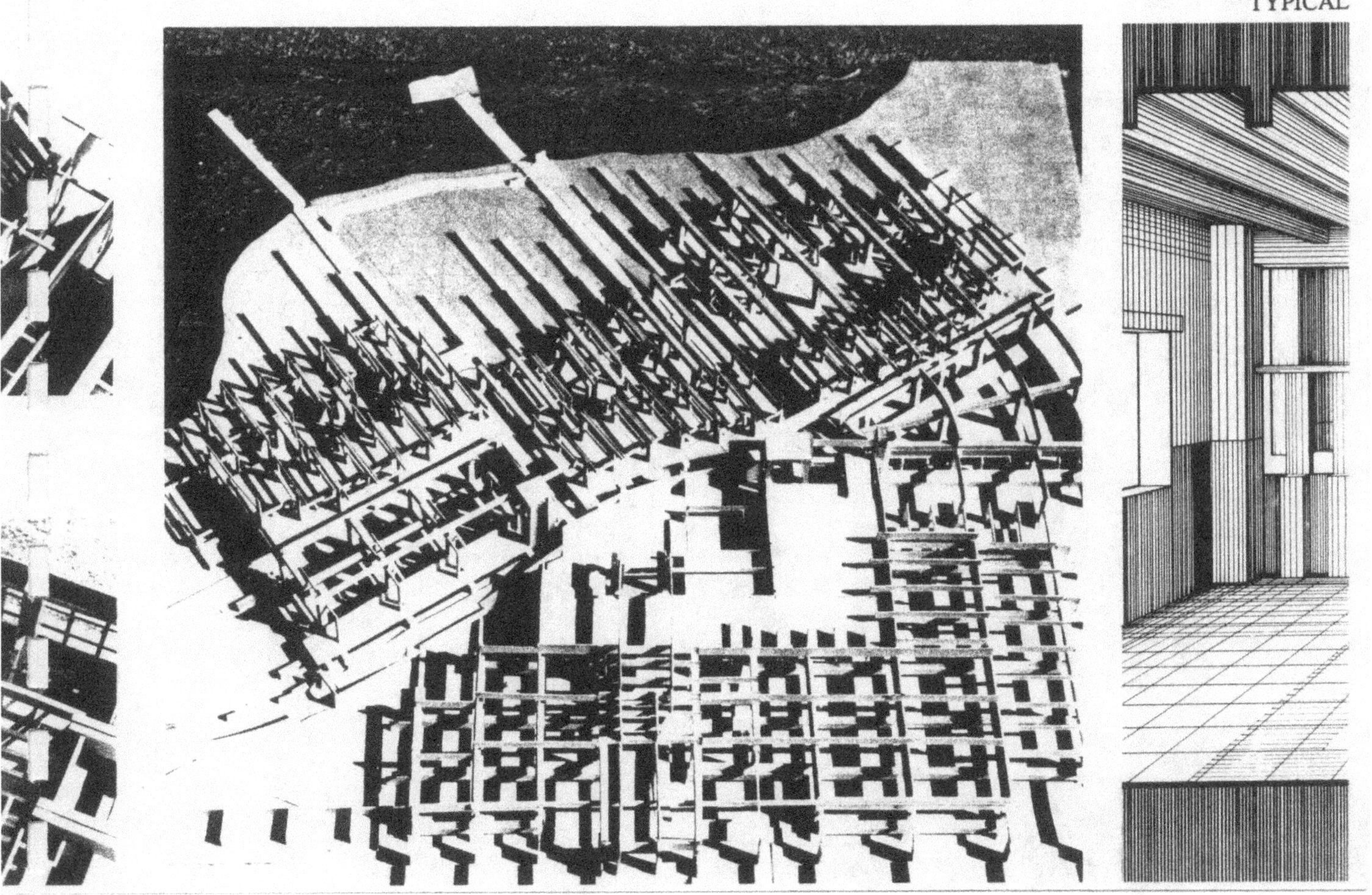
TYPICAL

APARTMENT INTERIOR

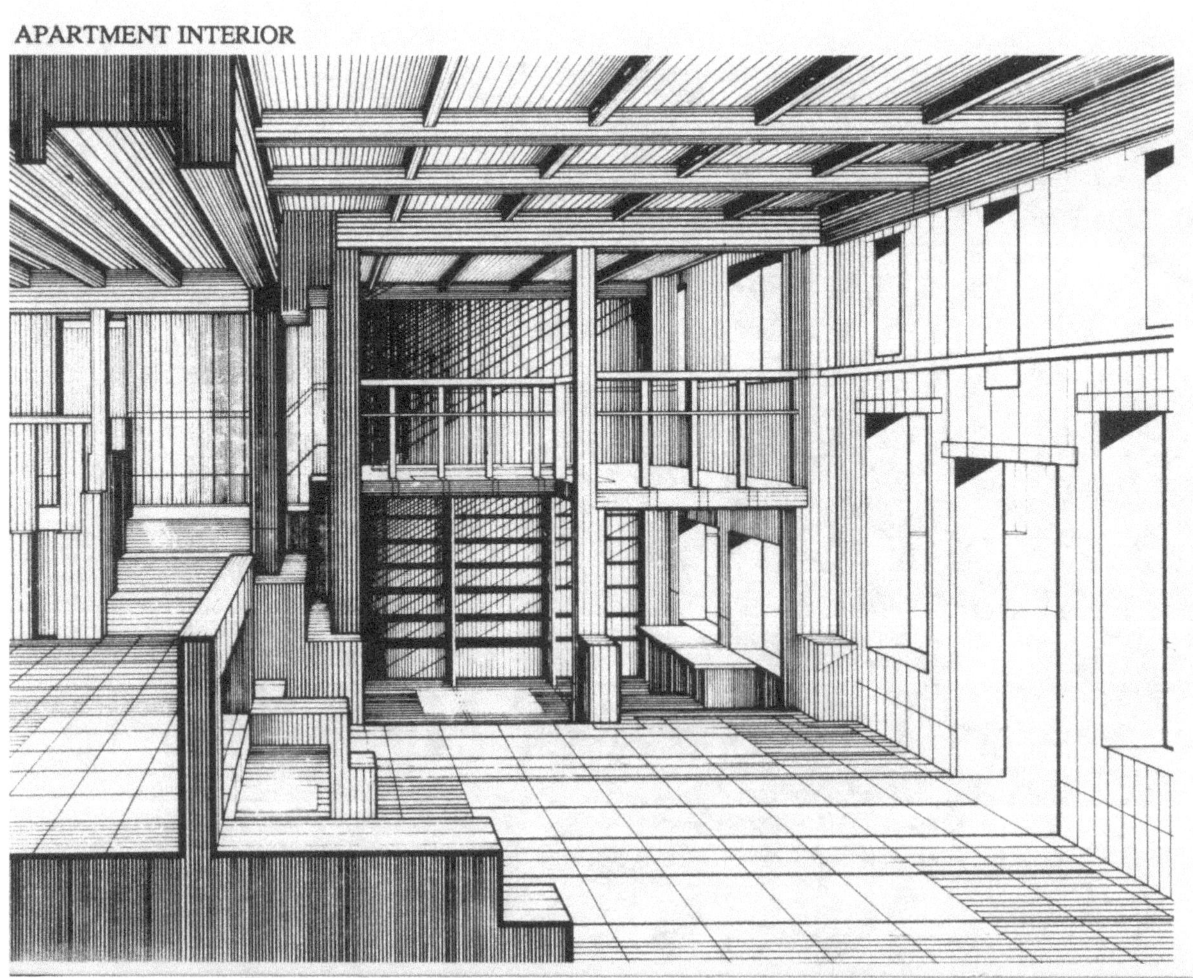

Savannah School of Design

Design 4

1987

I arrived at the design for this project through the study of Savannah's architectural typology which include the ideas of the square, the walled street, and the inherent duality in the Savannah house.

The Design School is sited on one of the set piece lots fronting Monterey Square. Thus the building has a definite front addressing the square and a back oriented towards one of the through-streets. The sides of the building where kept as solid as possible to address the street as a space without becoming oppressive. For example an arcade runs around the southwest corner of the building to mediate between street and built environment.

The Design School itself is conceived as a tri-partite scheme. An object surrounded by space (studios and galleries) and space carved out of an object (dorms and offices) separated by a meeting space (cafeteria) which in Savannah's typology becomes the separator between servant's housing and owner's quarters.

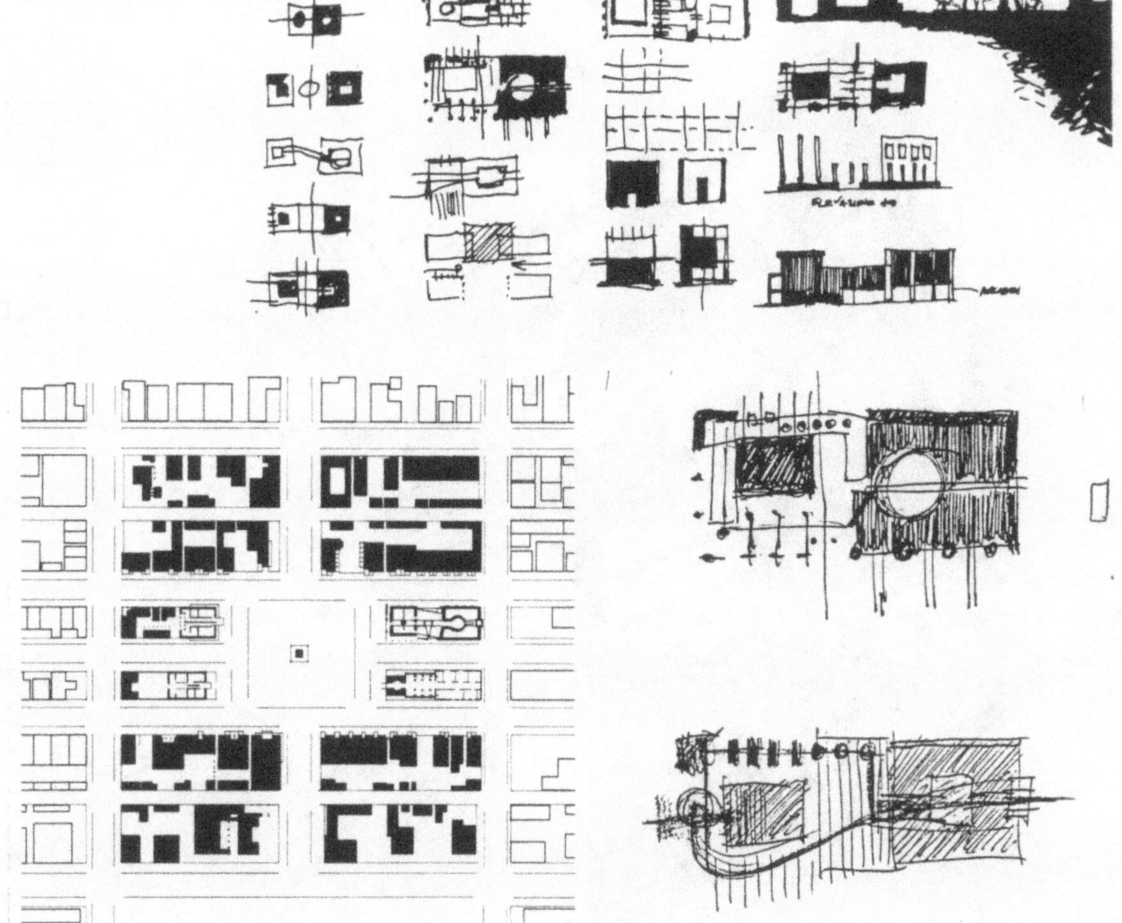

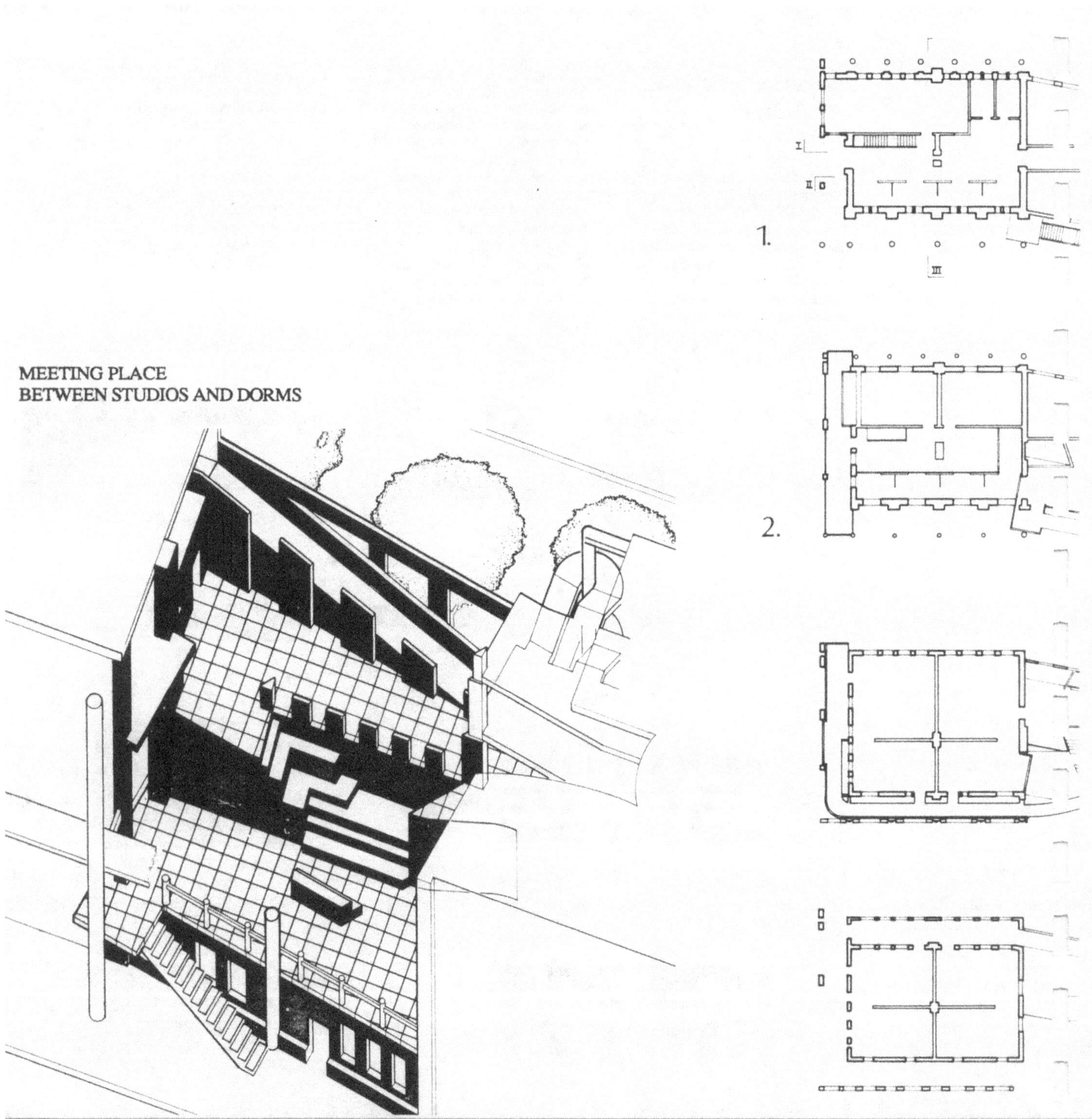
MEETING PLACE
BETWEEN STUDIOS AND DORMS
1.
2.
I
II
III

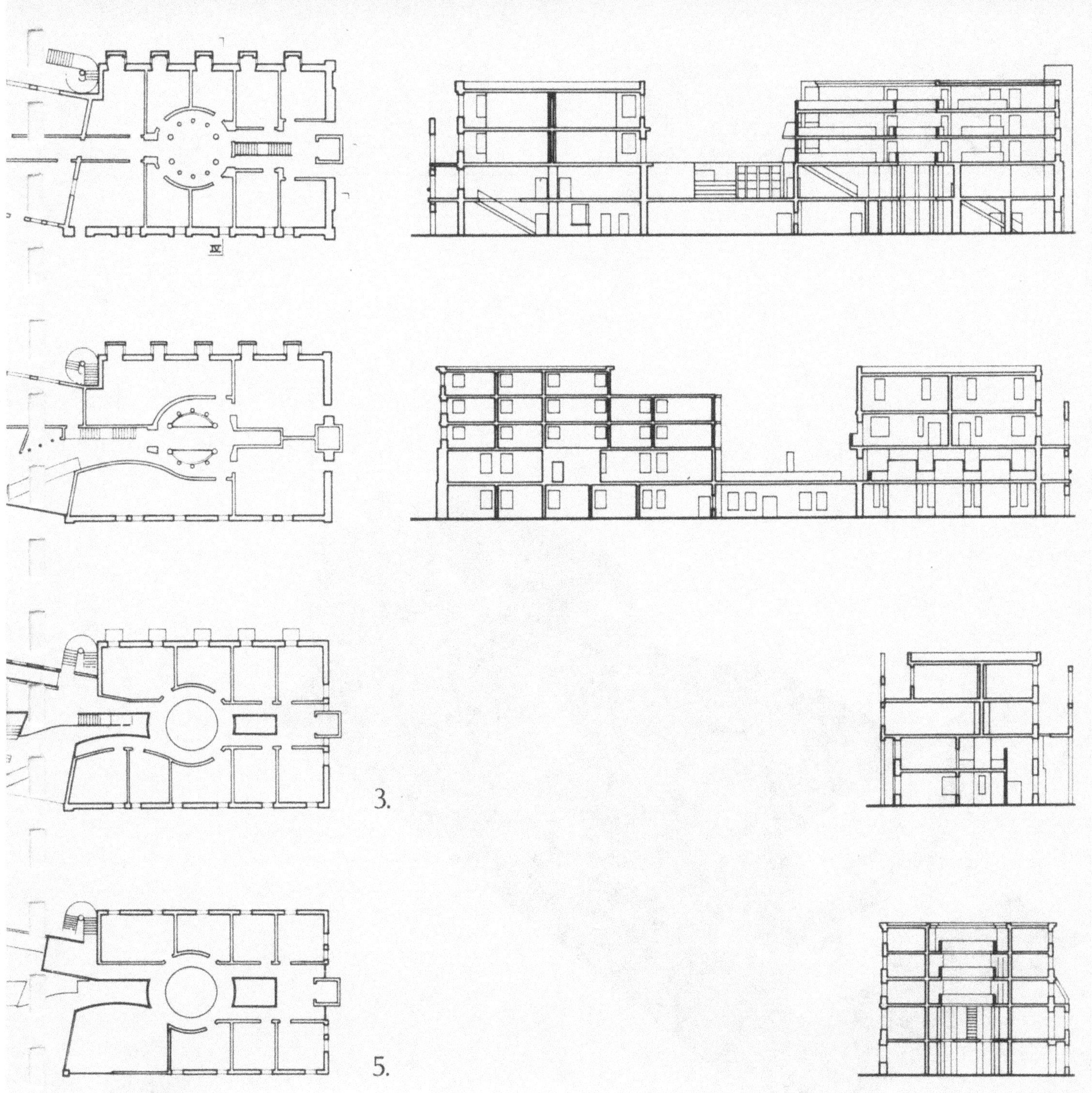
IV
3.
5.

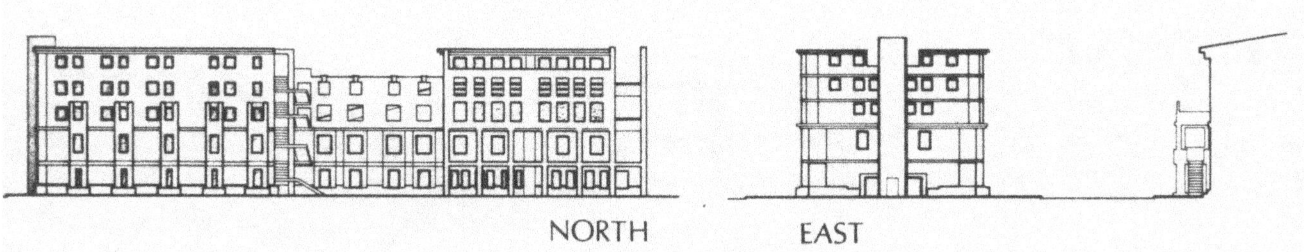
NORTH
EAST

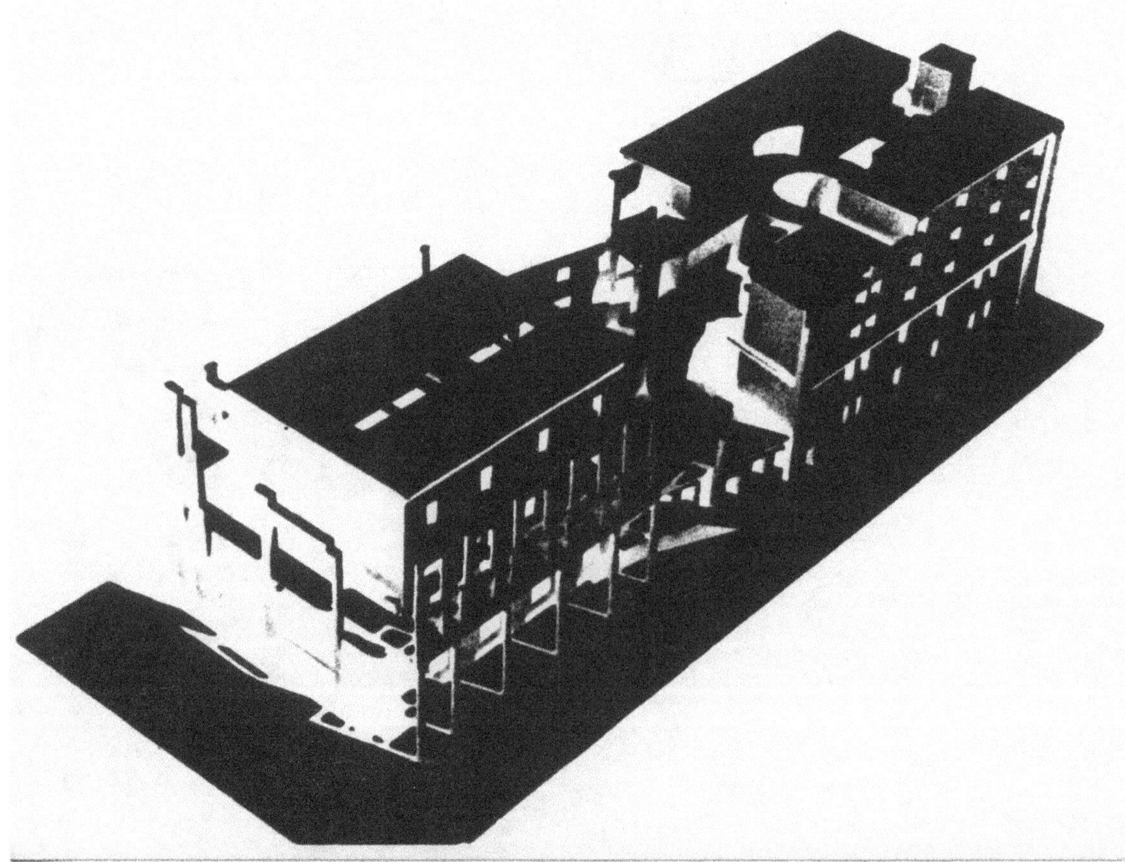

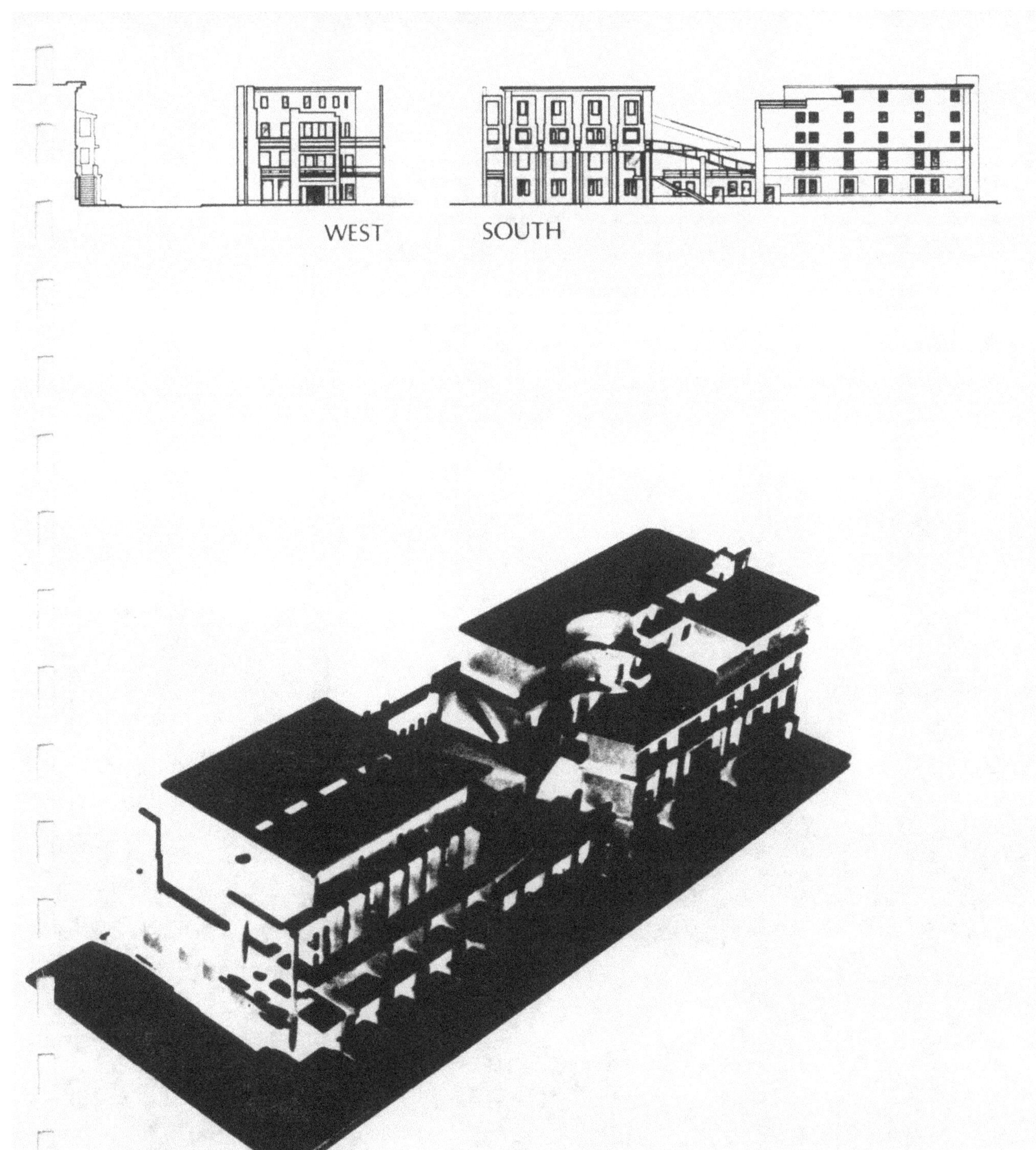
WEST
SOUTH

Viking Museum Chicago

Design 6

1988

This project attempts to create a space for the Gokstad, a Viking ship, buried about 1000 years ago, discovered in 1880 and a replica of it sailed to the Chicago World's Fair in 1893. Critical ideas dealt with the siting of the museum, the space for the ship itself and the geographical peculiarities of Norway.

The site is part of the 1893 World's Fair ground and presents approximately where the Gokstad replica landed in 1893. This brought up the idea of arrival but also the action of departure prior to arrival. The leaving of Norway by ship, sailing through a long and narrow fjord was transformed into a building of high walls or canyons that reflect the geography of Norway. The interior was conceived as an anti-climax to the Gokstad ship. A simple space to accentuate an elegant object. To prepare the visitor for this emotional experience he is subjected to spatial extremes by ascending along the blank face of the monumental north wall, turning and entering the actual building only to turn again and participate visually in the long exhibit space for the ship. On the south the building breaks down to a more human scale and relates to the Atlantic, the joint between Europe and America. This act of joining, the sailing of the Gokstad from Norway to Chicago is expressed by placing the museum at the most eastern edge of the site, addressing again the ideas of arrival and departure.

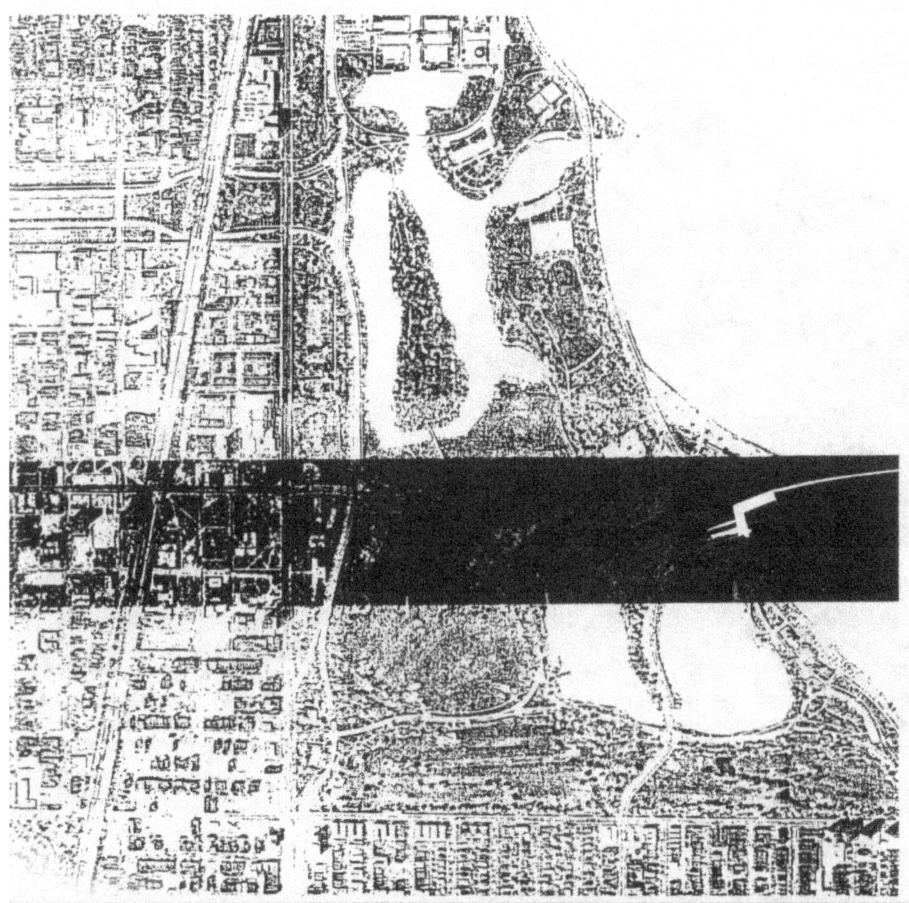

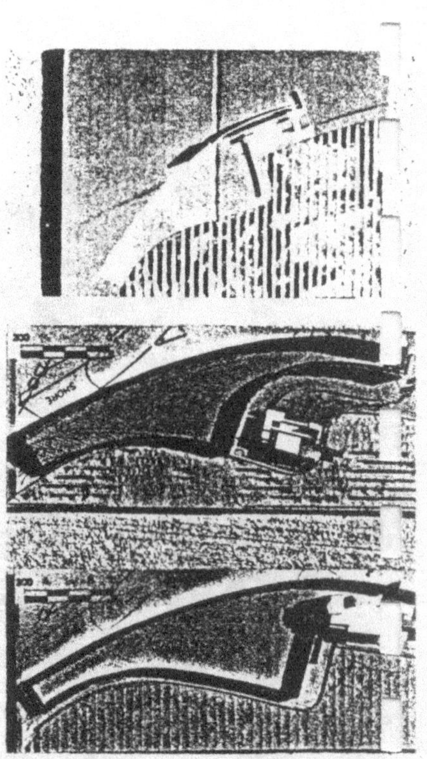

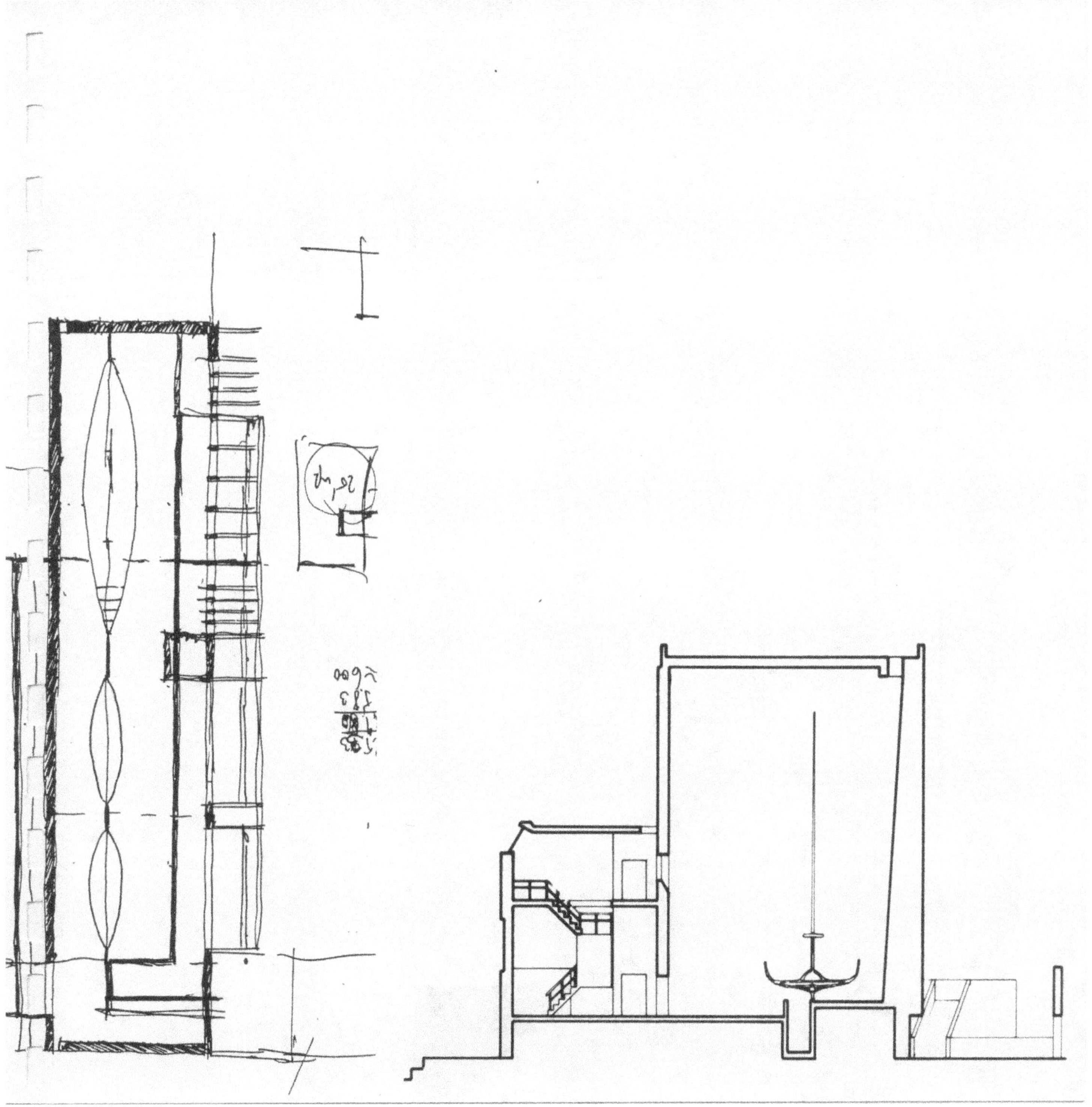

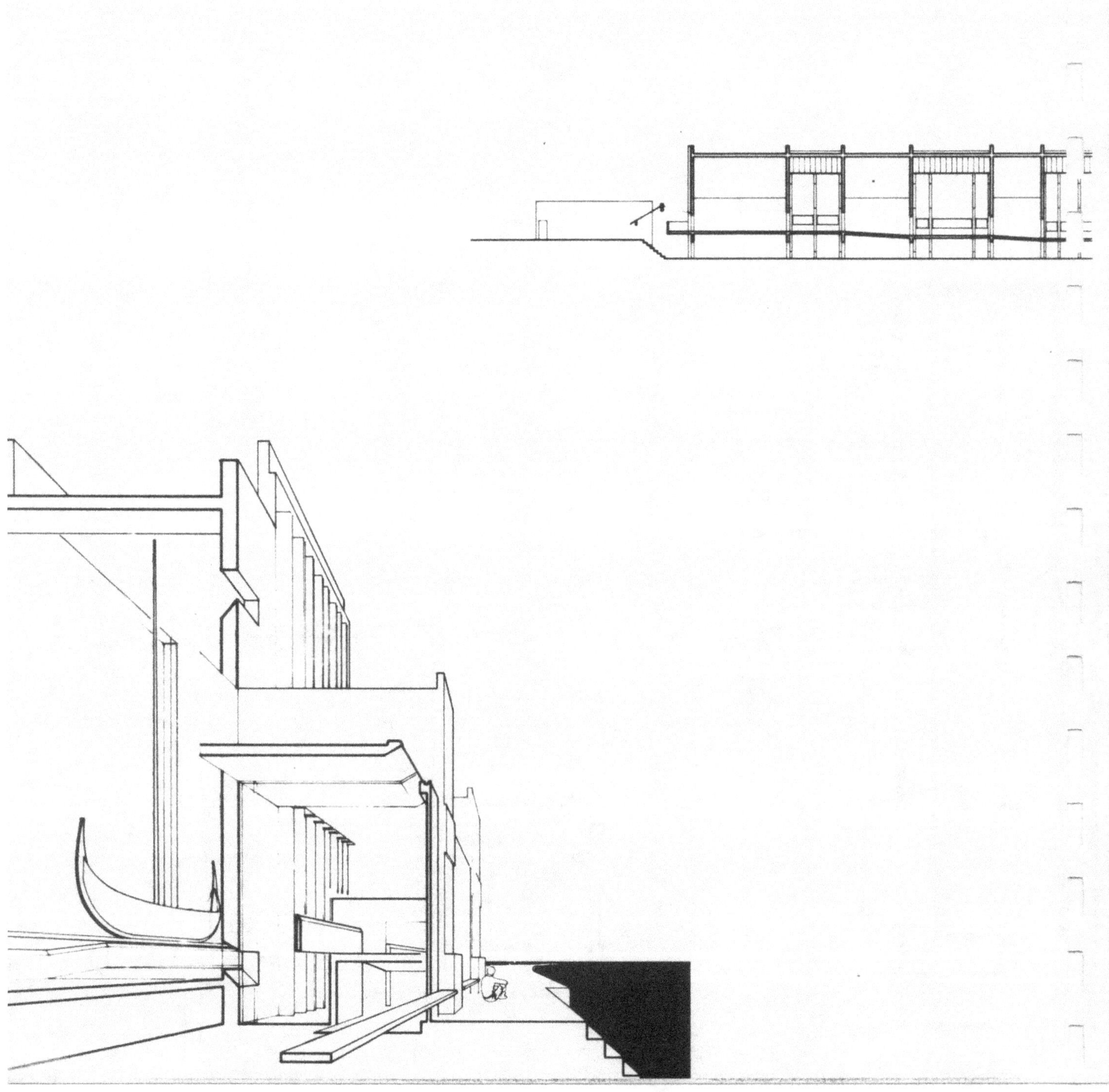

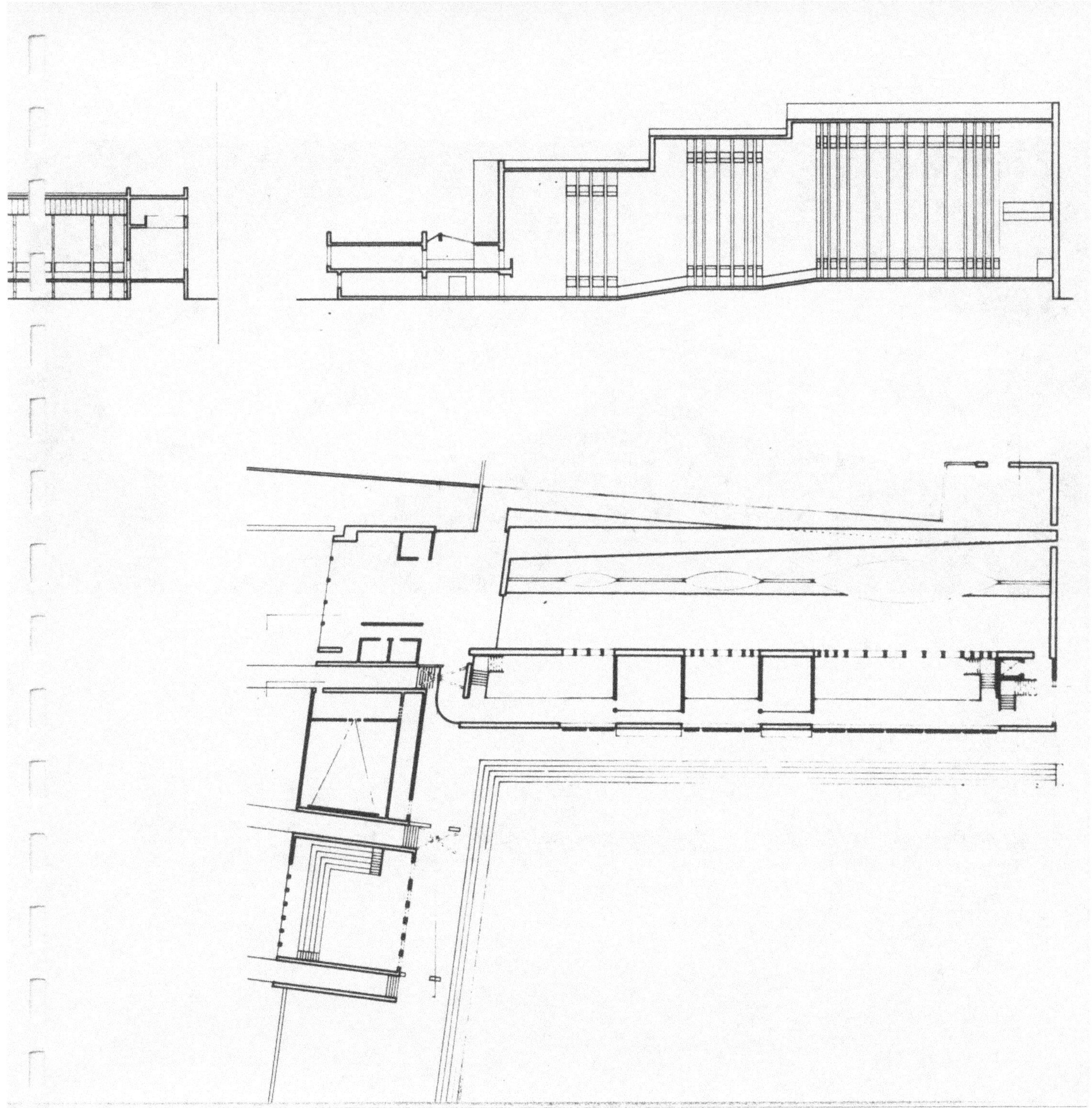

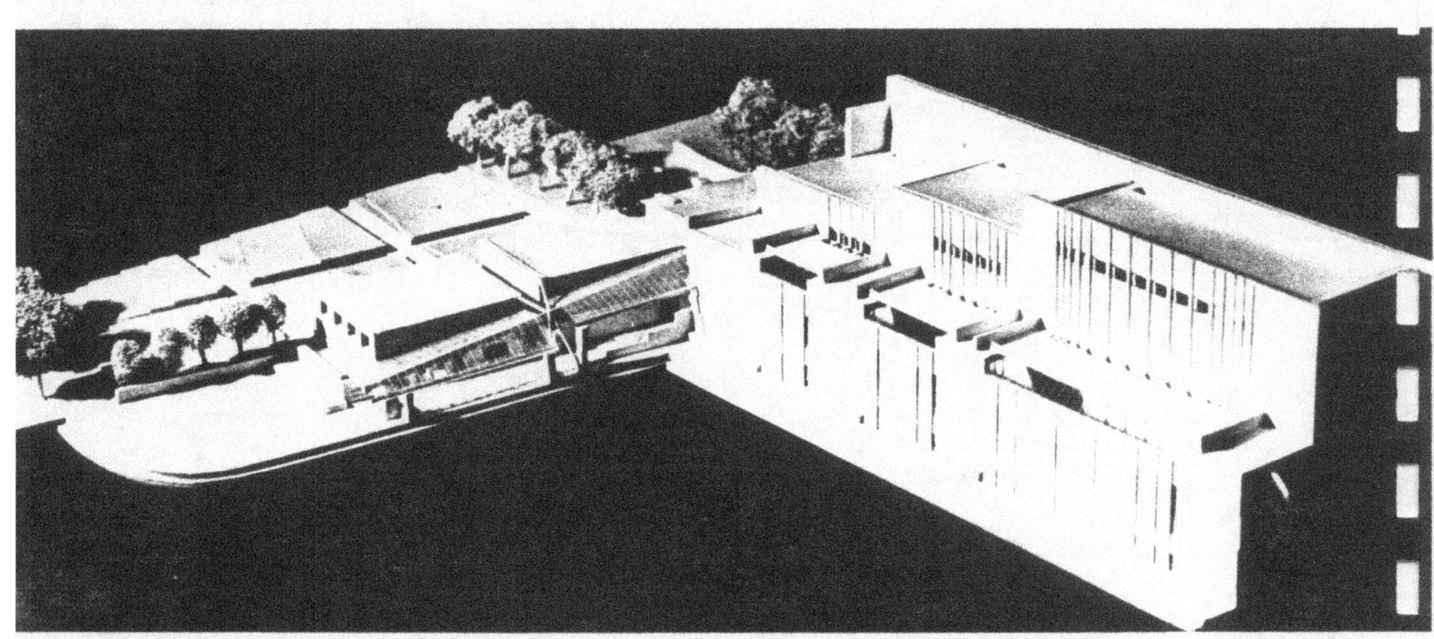

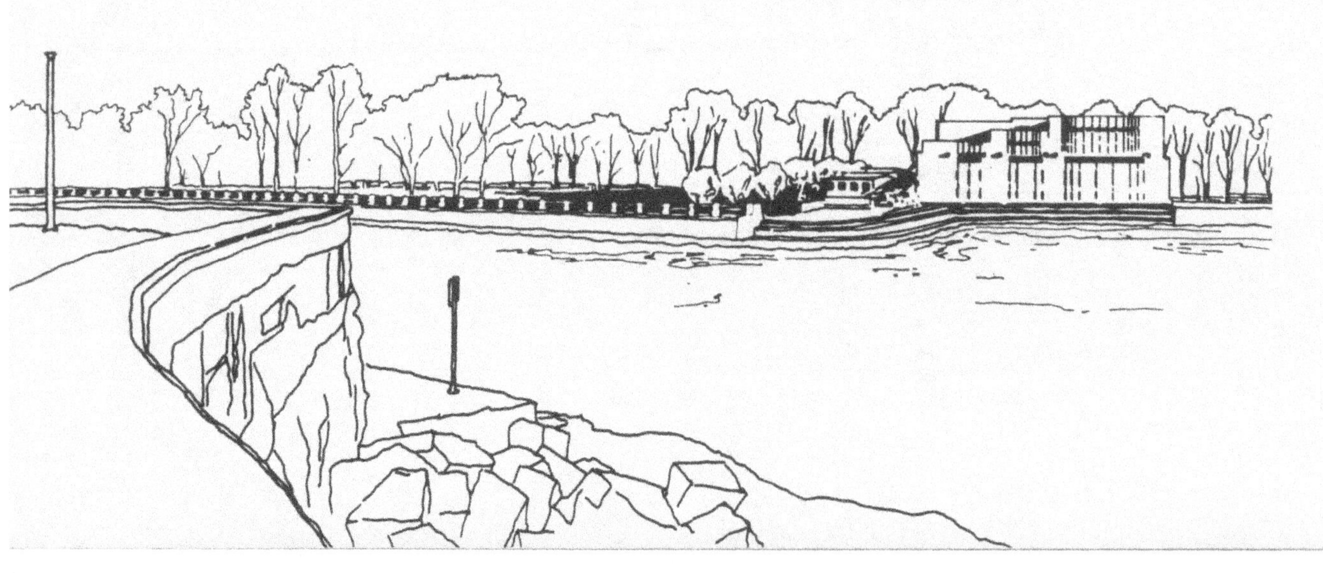

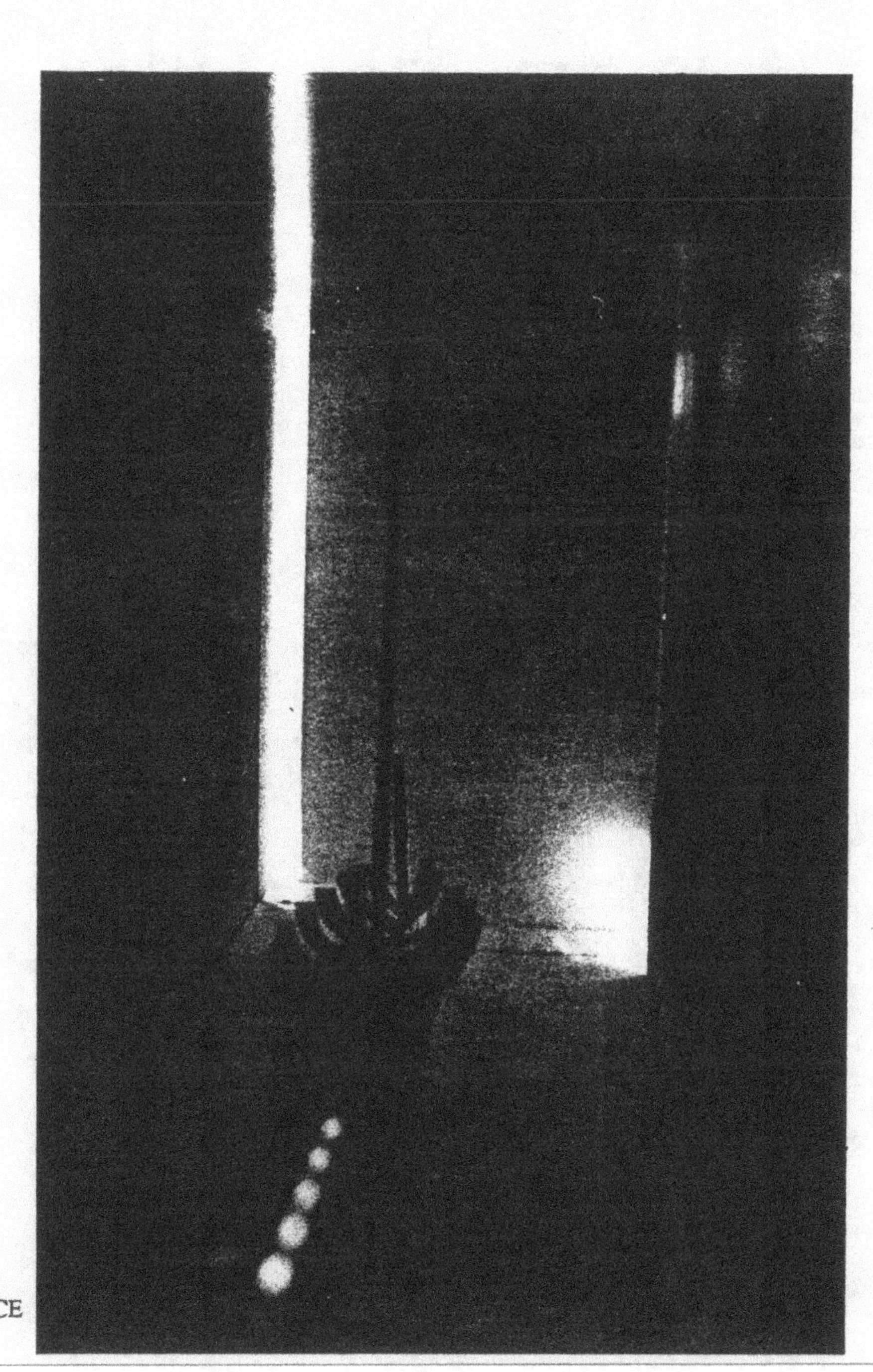

VIEW INTO
EXHIBIT SPACE

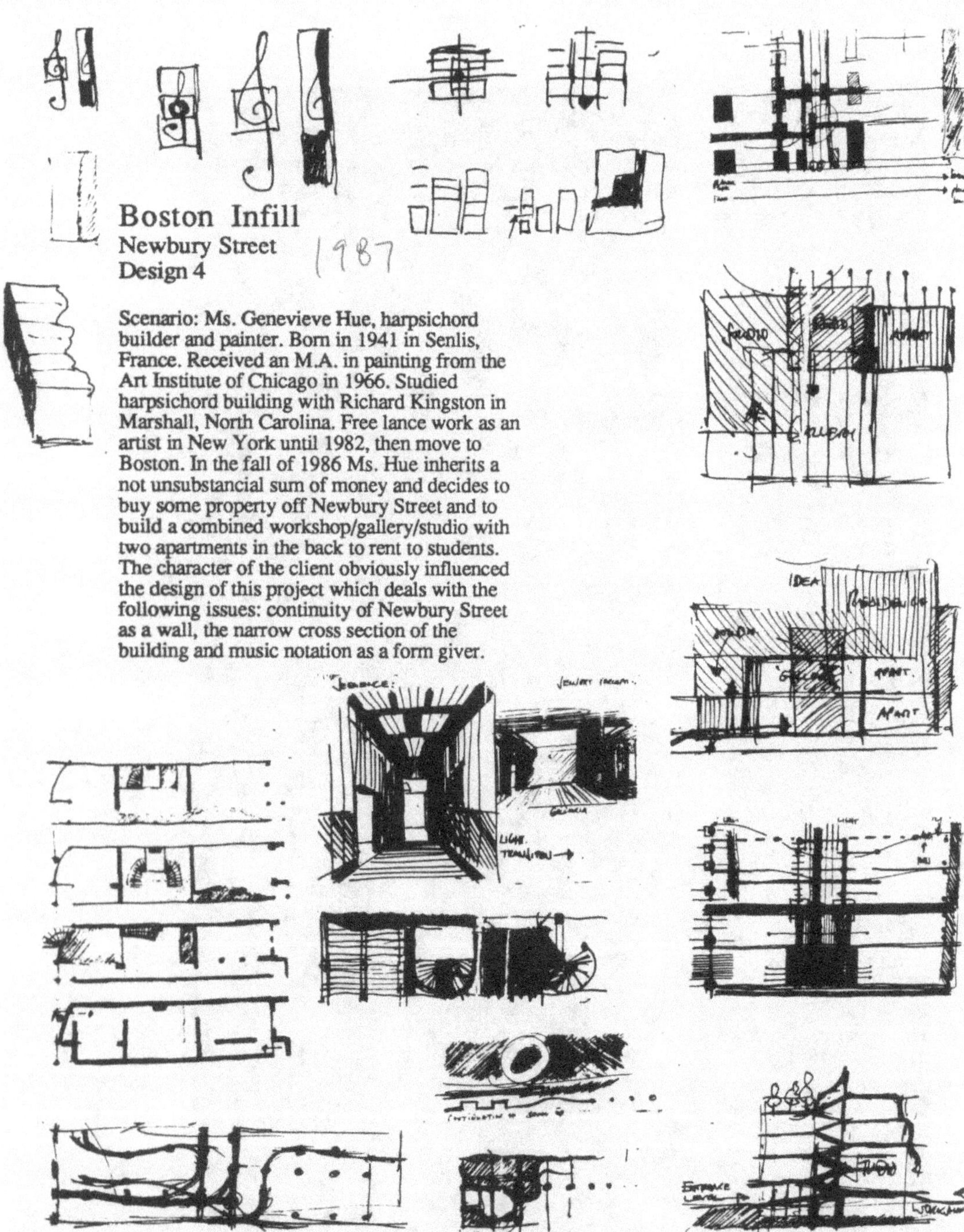

Boston Infill

Newbury Street 1987

Design 4

Scenario: Ms. Genevieve Hue, harpsichord builder and painter. Born in 1941 in Senlis, France. Received an M.A. in painting from the Art Institute of Chicago in 1966. Studied harpsichord building with Richard Kingston in Marshall, North Carolina. Free lance work as an artist in New York until 1982, then move to Boston. In the fall of 1986 Ms. Hue inherits a not unsubstancial sum of money and decides to buy some property off Newbury Street and to build a combined workshop/gallery/studio with two apartments in the back to rent to students. The character of the client obviously influenced the design of this project which deals with the following issues: continuity of Newbury Street as a wall, the narrow cross section of the building and music notation as a form giver.

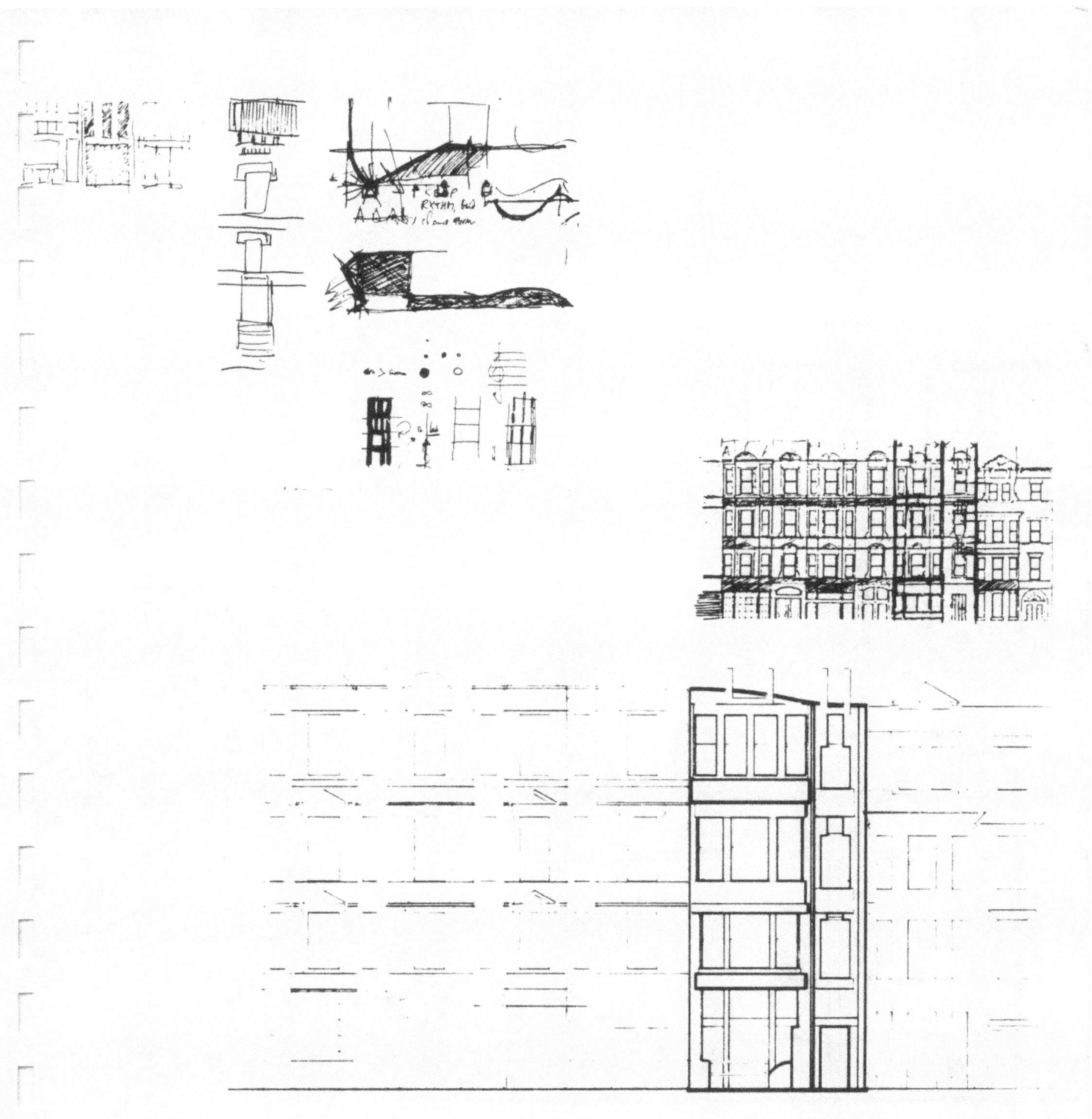

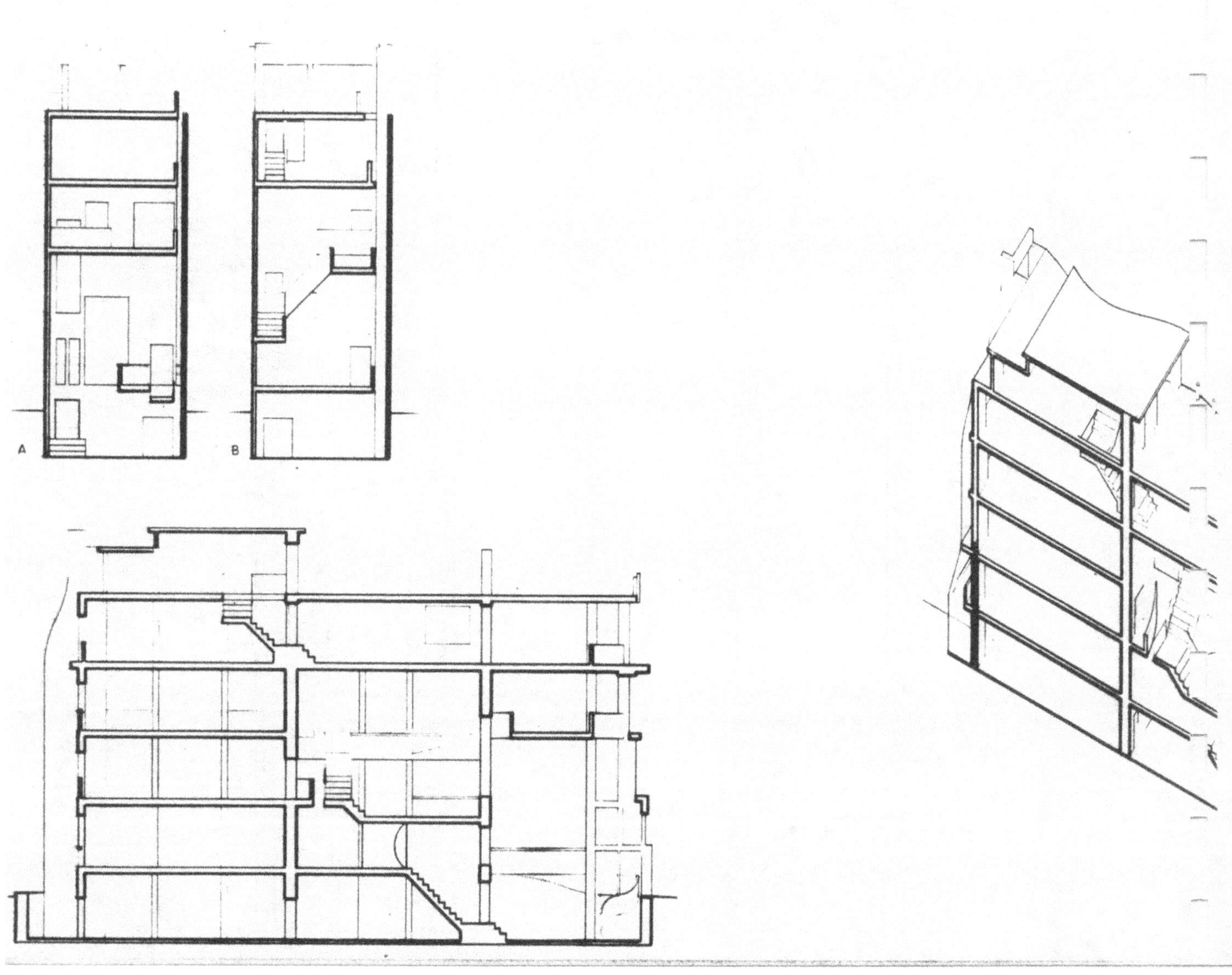
A
B

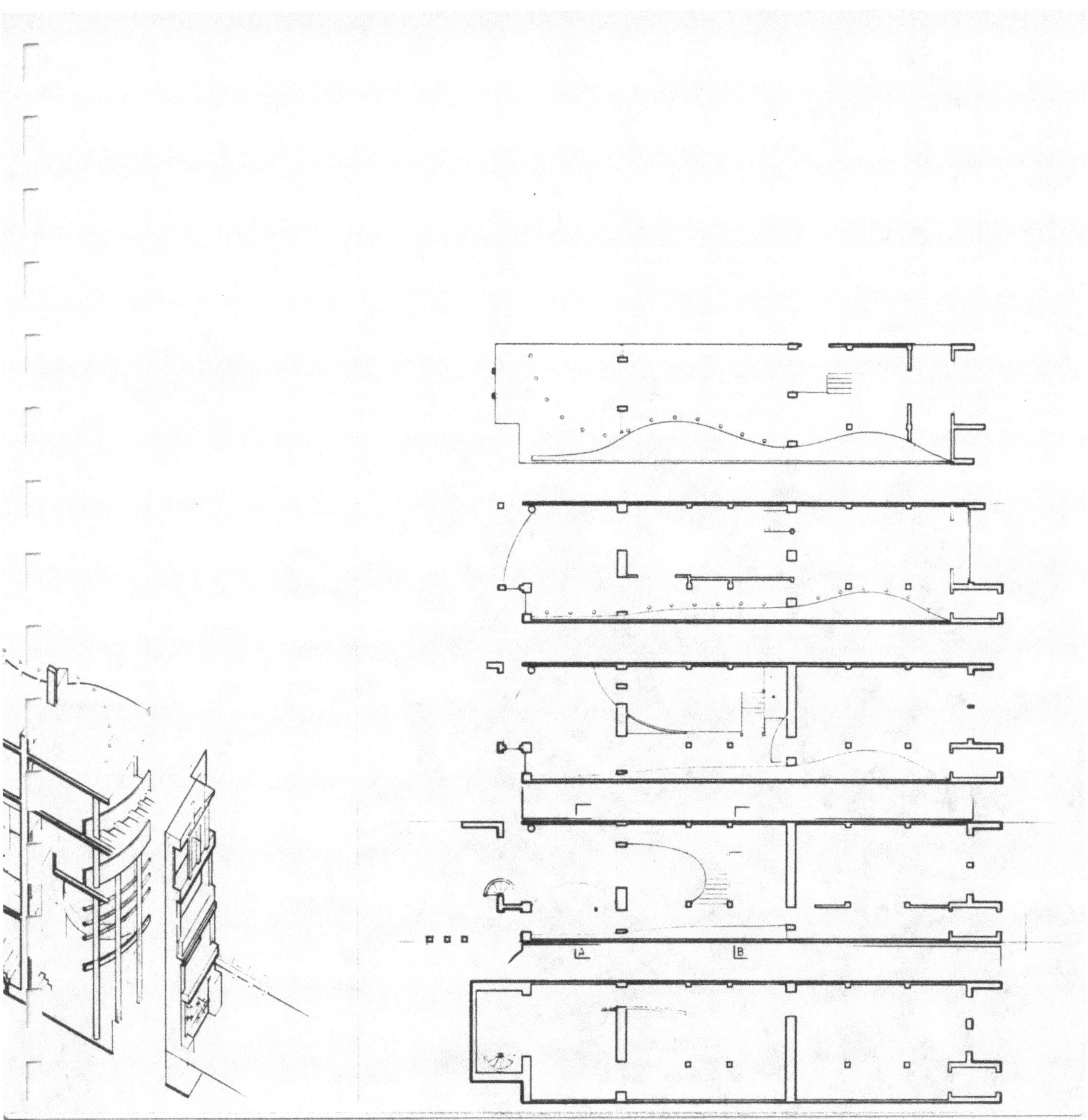

Boston Urban Design and Curley Library

1988

Design 7

Boston is about the absence of history. History in the sense of concealed layers (the german word for history is Geschichte= lit. layering). My design then is about an archeology of Boston where its citizens can reestablish their contact with an-other part of the city. I started by overlaying the existing city with a map from 1794.

Realizing the amount of artificial growth I decided to reverse the development of the land encroaching upon the water by cutting canals which terminate at the old coast line, into the existing fabric. Now the history of the city is more than the two-dimensional red line painted on the sidewalk; it becomes spatial and thus architectural.

In some parts the old coast line turns into buildings that are here not further defined. Another task in the urban design part of this project was to deal with the depression of the interstate artery that cuts the head of Boston in half. My strategy was to link the North End with the Government District, yet let

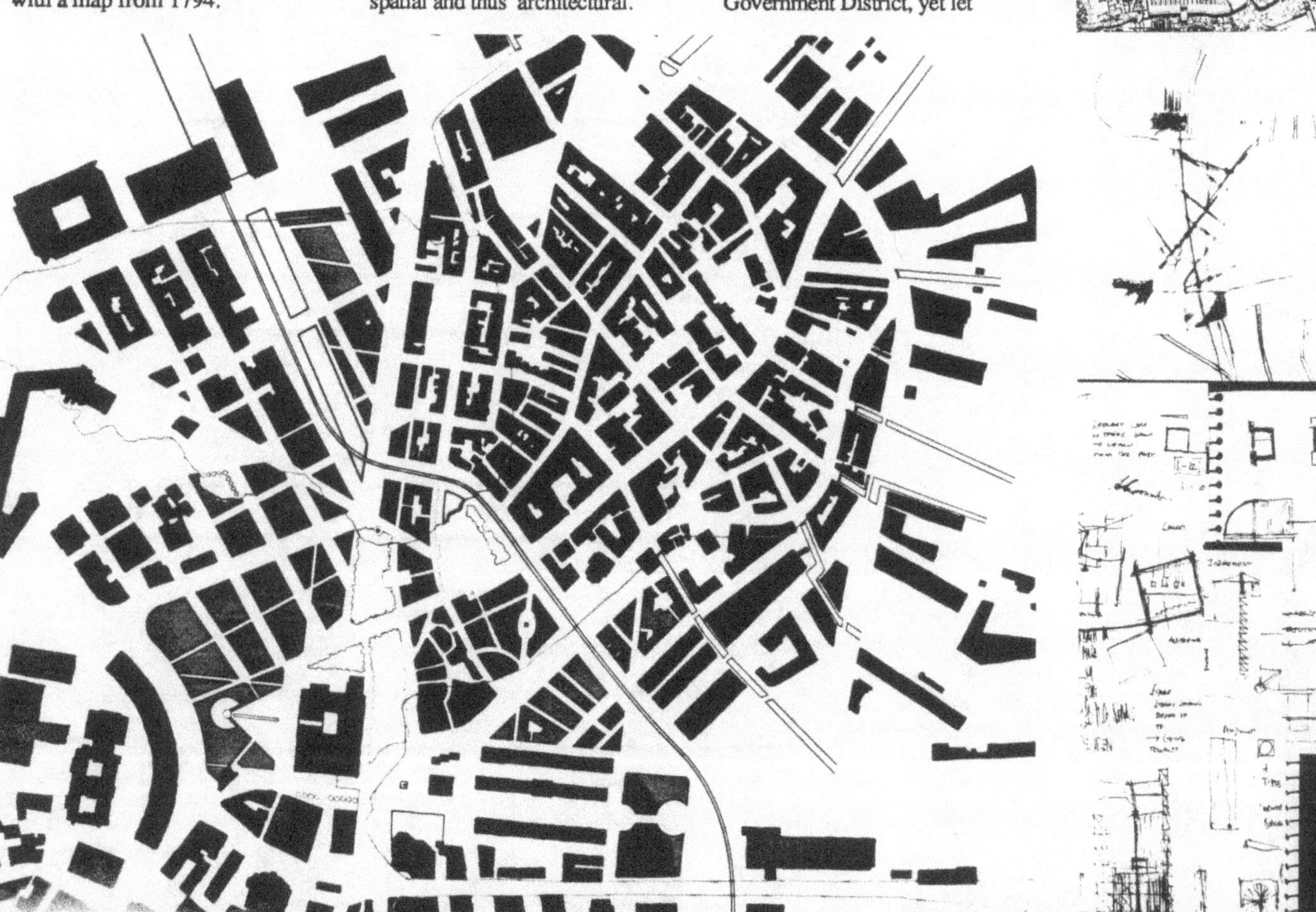

both of them keep their own identity through the insertion of the new Haymarket Square as a buffer in between. This square became also the site for the Curley Research Library.

In the library I am investigating the ideas and implications of time and ambiguity.
This library is a body of knowledge for researchers. Knowledge is aquired over time and is as such always incomplete, i.e. in a state of becoming. This ambiguity between becoming and being is expressed in the siting of the building. There is a dry moat surrounding the library, exposing the ancient layers in the ground, making entry possible only via a bridge that, when the library is closed, folds back and becomes part of the wall.

The program for the library also suggests a schism in that the largest part of the library is not accessible to the general public but only to researchers. Only the auditorium/gallery and the Curley Memorial Room can be entered by the public.
The two basement levels appropriately house the reserved stacks, the forbidden part of the library, the underground past, simultaneously exposed and hidden, accessible only by special permission. The open stacks share the two floors above ground level together with the entry piece and the Curley Memorial Room. The shifted cube above the open stacks is the reading room, one large volume whose edge is eaten away by the central vertical pendulum space which shows the reading room's dependency or for that matter everything's dependency on time. The tilted and shifted gallery/auditorium at the top of the library symbolize the current state of confusion and instability in the body of knowledge.
The truss houses the elevator, a tentative link. Towering above everything else is the crane, symbol of change in every city.

row of tall buildings
grey sky with thin trusses;
cranes
that don't fly anymore

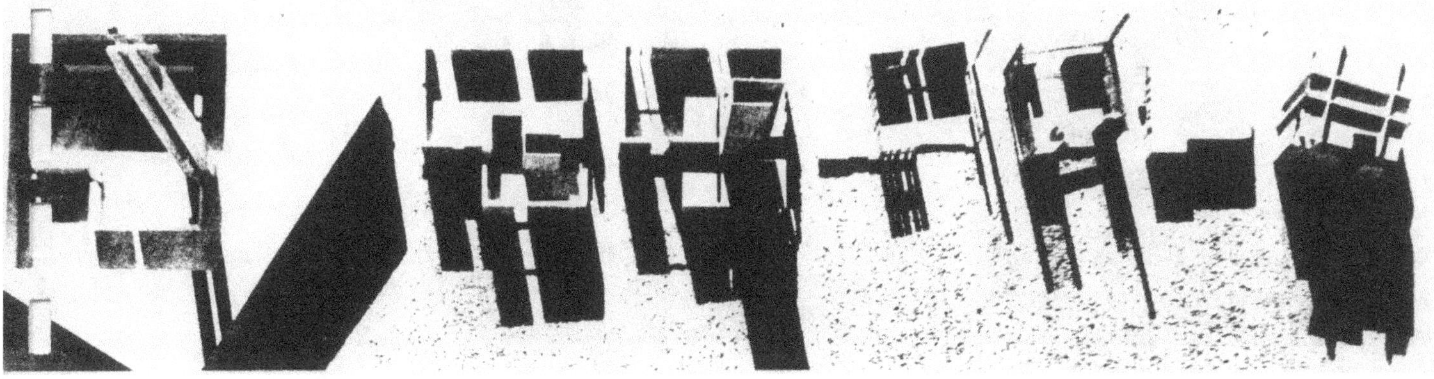

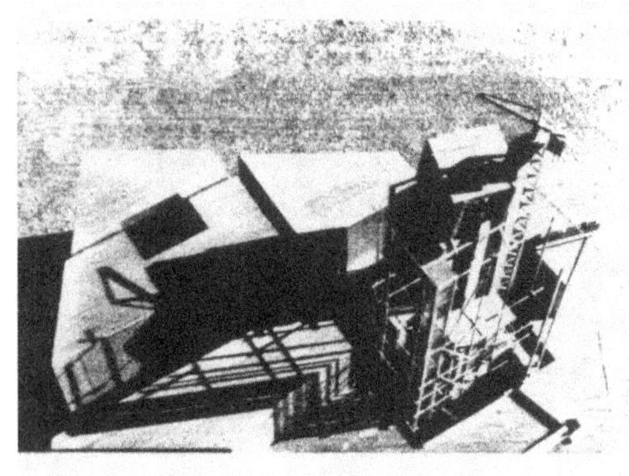
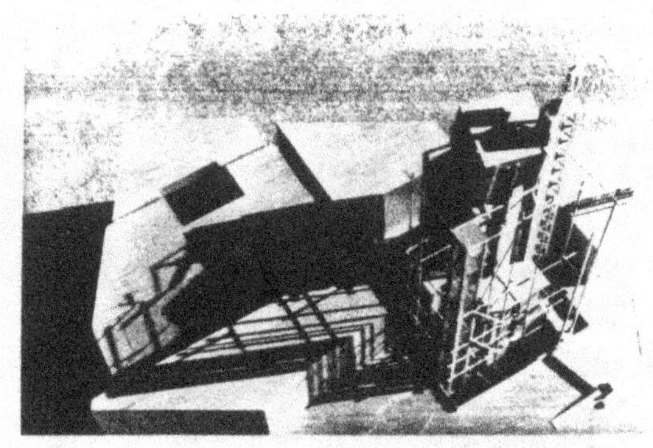
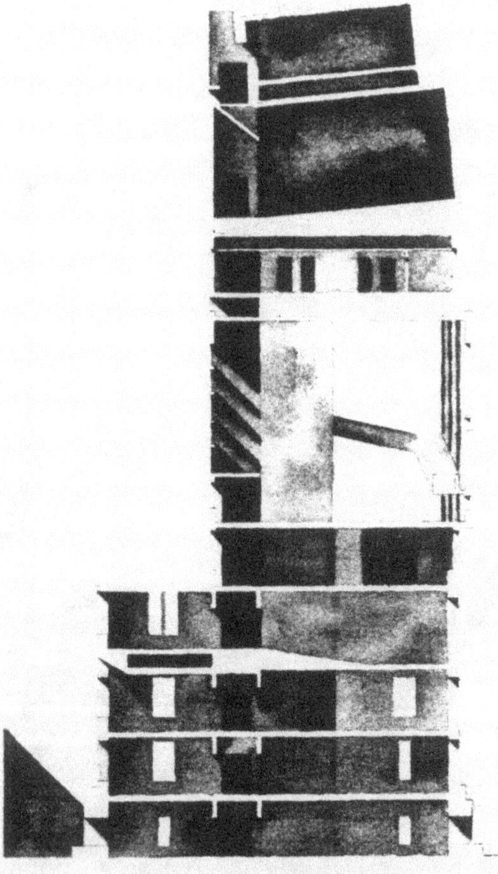
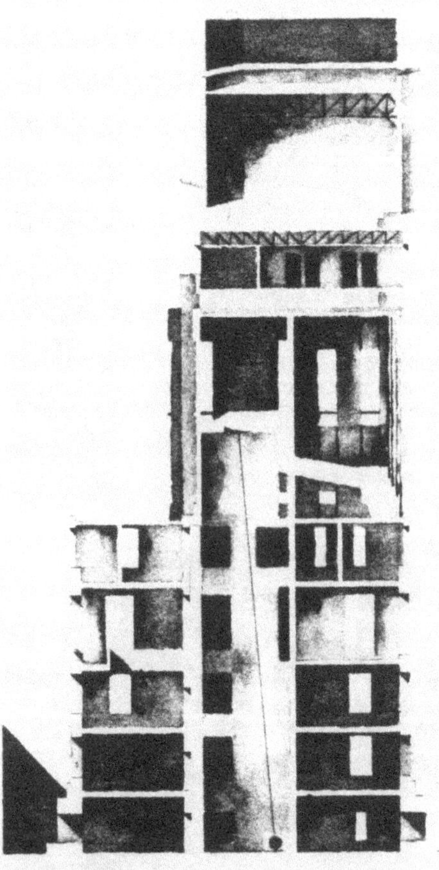

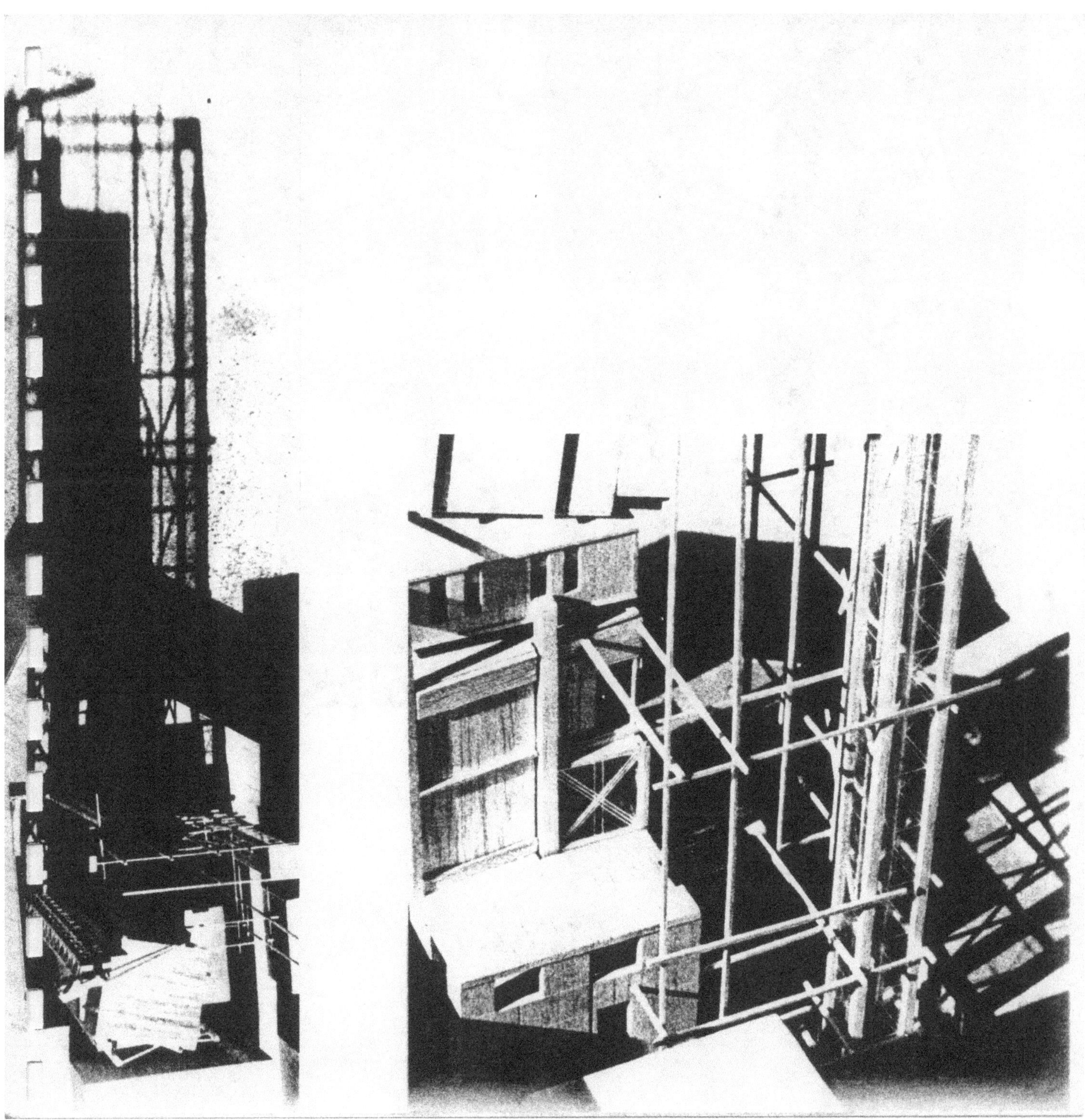

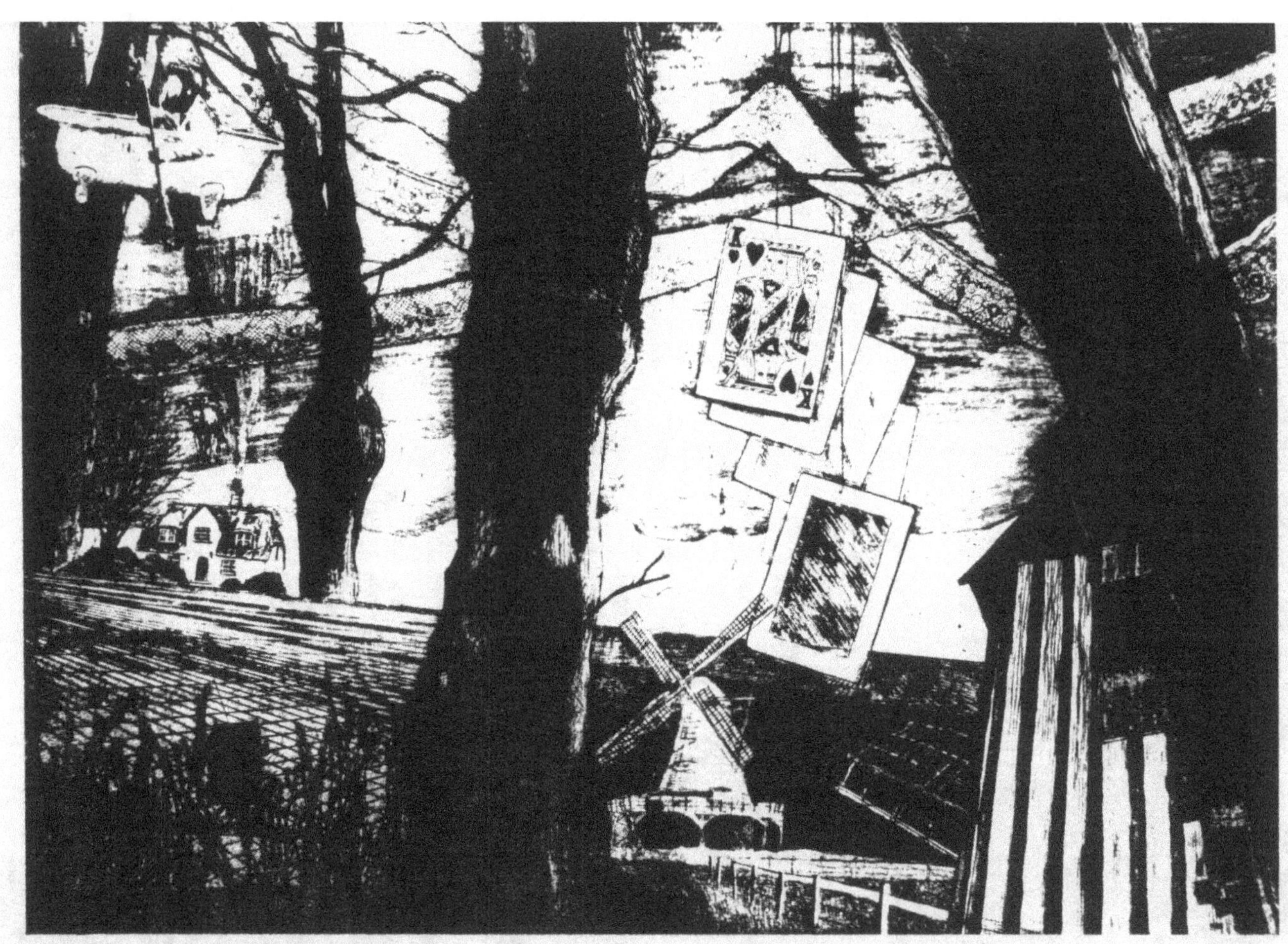

'DUKE OF CLUBS'
ETCHING AND AQUATINT ON COPPER PLATE
SUMMER 1988

PHOTOGRAPH
VENICE, ITALY
SUMMER 1988

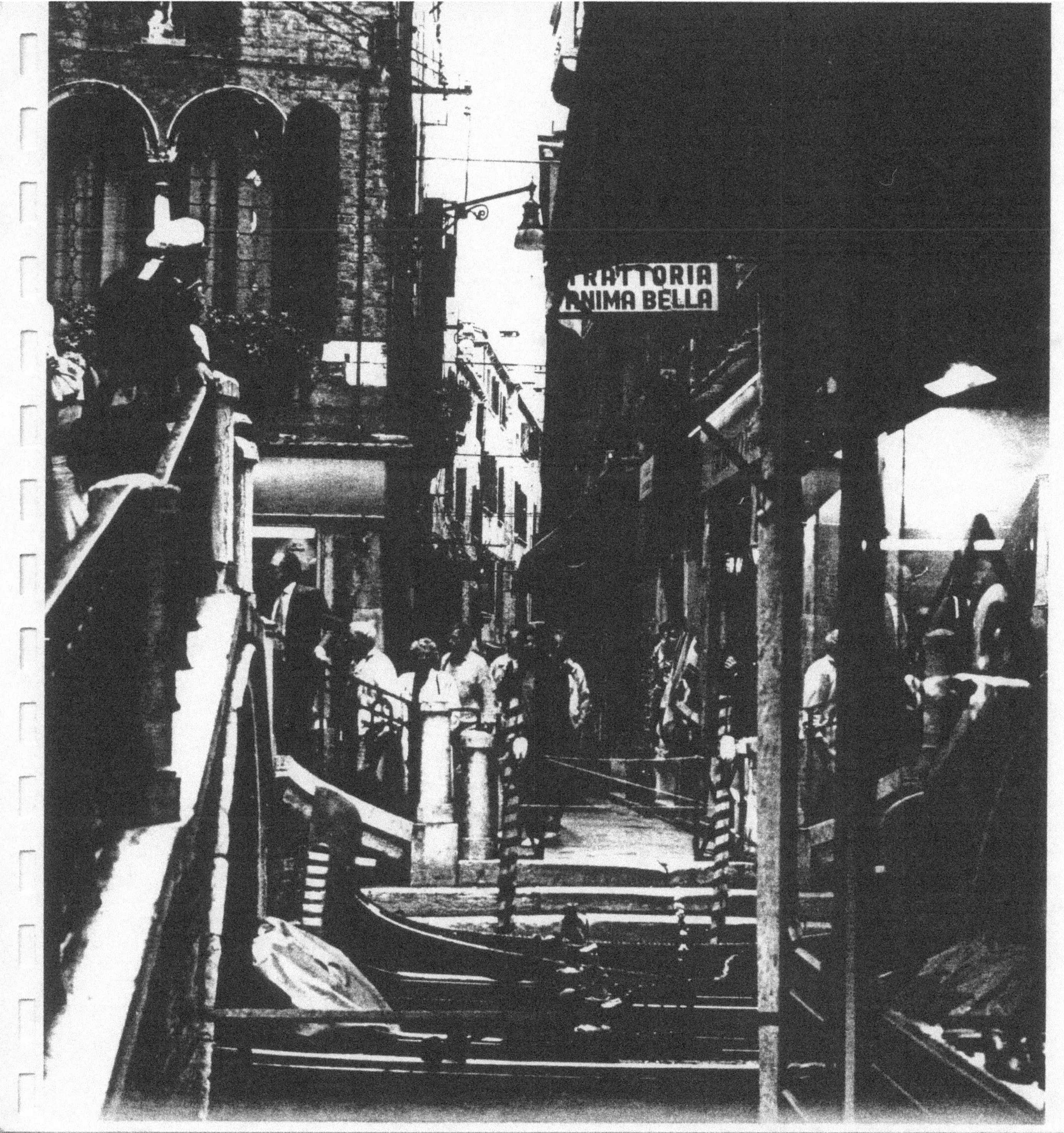
RATTORIA
NIMA BELLA

www.ingramcontent.com/pod-product-compliance
Lightning Source LLC
LaVergne TN
LVHW080337110826

845155LV00027B/253
9781941892343